TILLER:

NOT YOUR AVERAGE JOE

JOE TILLER
WITH TOM KUBAT

SportsPublishingLLC.com

ISBN-10: 1-59670-032-7
ISBN-13: 978-1-59670-032-1

Publishers: Peter L. Bannon and Joseph J. Bannon Sr.
Senior managing editor: Susan M. Moyer
Acquisitions editor: Mike Pearson
Developmental editor: Travis W. Moran
Art director: K. Jeffrey Higgerson
Dust jacket design: Joseph Brumleve
Interior layout: Dustin J. Hubbart
Photo editor: Erin Linden-Levy

Sports Publishing L.L.C.
804 North Neil Street
Champaign, IL 61820
Phone: 1-877-424-2665
Fax: 217-363-2073
SportsPublishingLLC.com

Printed in the United States of America

Library of Congress Cataloging-in-Publication Data

Tiller, Joe, 1942-
    Tiller : not your average Joe / Joe Tiller with Tom Kubat.
    p. cm.
    ISBN-13: 978-1-59670-032-1 (hard cover : alk. paper)
    ISBN-10: 1-59670-032-7 (hard cover : alk. paper)
    1. Tiller, Joe, 1942- 2. Football coaches--United States--Biography.
3. Purdue University--Football. 4. Purdue Boilermakers (Football team) I. Kubat, Tom, 1945- II. Title.
GV939.T494A3 2006
793.332092--dc22
    [B]
                            2006030848

To my, wife, Arnette, for believing in me, for her dedication to our family, and for sharing my dreams—you are my best friend.

To our three children, Renee, Julie, and Mike, who I love more than they'll ever know, probably more than I ever showed. They all light up my life.

CONTENTS

FOREWORD

BY JOE PATERNO
PENN STATE UNIVERSITY HEAD FOOTBALL COACH

C oach Tiller and I first met by accident years ago, waiting to make connections in the Dallas airport. Planes were having trouble getting in and out, so we were stuck there for a couple of hours. I was having a drink when Joe came over and introduced himself. I believe he was at Wyoming at the time, and I took a liking to him right away because he wasn't one of those guys trying to impress anybody.

Then we really didn't see each other until he got the job at Purdue. Joe entered the Big Ten Conference with a very sophisticated, well-organized, and disciplined passing game. Some people doubted whether he could bring a passing game into the Big Ten because of the weather—that it was too cold and too windy, that it snowed in the Midwest. I got a kick out of his reaction when he first arrived at Purdue and was asked about the impact weather conditions would have on his spread offense.

"Don't you think it snows in Wyoming?" he would say.

When Coach Tiller took over the Purdue program, he really transformed the Big Ten. At that time, we were dominated by people who thought, in order to be successful, all you had to do was jam the ball down everybody's throat. Joe had a lot of success very quickly because he knew what he was doing. He didn't have the greatest athletes, but they made a big impact on the whole league. Pretty soon everybody in the Big Ten was throwing the ball all over the place, trying to keep up with them.

Through the Big Ten coaches meetings and other outings, we've been able to spend some time together and get to know each other. One thing I've learned is that Joe is always in good humor. I had a pretty good football team when we played Purdue one year, led by a kid named Curtis Enis at running back. We won that game, and afterwards, when we met at midfield, Joe said to me, "Going into this game I wondered whether you had a good football team, I wondered whether you were a good coach, and I wondered whether you had a great player. I don't know about the first two, but you did have a great player."

Talking with Penn State coach Joe Paterno before our game against the Nittany Lions at Purdue in 2005. He was complimenting me on my Wyoming-style necktie. Photo provided courtesy of the Journal-Courier (Lafayette, Indiana)

All the things I like and respect in coaching—that hopefully you will have a significant, meaningful impact on a young man when he's 18, 19, 20, or 21—is what Joe represents. The good coaches always manage to keep things in perspective, and Joe has done that. I would think if you're a kid, an intelligent kid, he'd be the kind of guy for whom you'd want to play. He doesn't give you a lot of horse manure. He just says, "Hey, this is my program. Come on in and you'll get a fair shake."

His teams always play hard, and very rarely do you see his kids showboat or take cheap shots. They play hard, they play smart, and it's fun to play them. Sometimes you wish his team wasn't as good—or that you weren't being out-coached by him—but I think Joe's really what college coaching is all about. He's not a hypocrite; he doesn't cheat; he's as honest as can be; and he's a great football coach. And you can underline the word *great*.

ACKNOWLEDGMENTS

A special thanks to the sports information staffs at Montana State University, Washington State University, the University of Wyoming, and Purdue University for their assistance in providing photos and related information for this book. Thanks to my family— my wife, Arnette; children, Renee, Julie, and Mike; my brothers, Chuck, Fred, Marvin, and sister, Janet Miller. They are truly the 'A' Team.

Over the years, I have been associated with a number of teams that were all special in their own way. Nearly all I've learned has come from the players and coaches on those teams. As I've often stated, "It's their world—I'm just passing through." What a great trip they have made it.

An unprecedented thanks goes to the secretaries with whom I've had the pleasure of working. They have kept me sane and on task throughout my entire coaching career. Without their patience and understanding, I would have crashed long ago.

Finally, to everyone who ever played a role in the teams I've been a part of, they have contributed to the success of anything we've accomplished. I'm referring to support staffs, administrators, fans, and friends—thank you all.

Chapter 1

COLLOMORE ROAD

When the school bell rang at Little Flower Grade School, a Catholic school run by Franciscan nuns, I would run to get into the proper line. They taught not three 'Rs' but four—*reading, 'riting, 'rithmatic, and regimentation.* Along with a stern dose of discipline, these were our staples. The nuns would crack the backs of your fingers with a ruler if you were out of line. Hardly anyone crossed that line more than once, although I did maybe twice. Despite that discipline, I really looked forward to the fall and the beginning of the school year, which brought the start of football season and meant that I could play on the neighborhood little guy team. We were called the Reynolds Corners Panthers—a renegade community team comprised of kids from different grade schools, a team with no age or weight restrictions. One year our team was pretty good because we had a big running back everyone was afraid to tackle. I finally figured out why this guy was such a terror. He drove to the games. He was in the eighth grade, but he was 16 and old enough to drive.

I'm not sure of the year, but this photo had to be one of the first of me—probably my first birthday!
Photo provided by the Joe Tiller family

Competing against teams from the CYO (Catholic Youth Organization) and some of the other elementary schools on the west side of Toledo, Ohio, I guess you could say we were a football version of the Bad News Bears. We'd go door to door trying to raise money and get some of the local businesses, whose names would be on our jerseys, to sponsor us. Since we had multiple sponsors, each jersey was different aside from the base color.

I didn't have any football shoes, so I wore my oldest brother's old, worn-out shoes. The doggone washers that held the cleats in place would chew up my socks and then the bottom of my feet. Before long, I began putting cardboard insoles in those shoes, but I had to replace them about every other day. Because they were too big, I also had to put cotton in the toes of the shoes to keep them on my feet—my humble introduction to organized football.

We'd go over to the coach's house and all the shoulder pads would be strewn about the living room, and he'd say, "Grab a pair there, Joe, and see if something fits you." First come, first serve, so you always tried to get there early for a decent helmet—one that fit with less than two fingers' space between your head and the padding.

I joined the Reynolds Corners Panthers when I was in the fifth grade. Because I was the littlest guy on the team, I'd dress out, but I didn't play. I don't remember doing much at practice those early days besides watching and running wind sprints at the end. Adjacent to our playing field was a grocery store, Palms Dairy, which eventually became my sponsor. On the side of the store was a spigot, and three or four of us had to take cases of pint bottles in a wire basket to the store, fill them up with water, and bring them back for the guys who were playing. We were like glorified water boys, but in uniform. One game, one of my uncles was coming to see me play, and I was so excited. Yet, when he came out, I was walking up with those water bottles.

"Hey, Joey—how you doing?" he said innocently, but I was so embarrassed. I never got to play in that game.

The 1954 Reynolds Corners Panthers. I'm in the back row, the last player on the far right, standing next to our coach, Mr. Bob Biedleman. My college roommate-teammate, Dan Wheeler, is in the second row, seventh from the left. Photo provided by the Joe Tiller family

I don't remember playing the next year either, for that matter. I finally got to play when I was in the seventh and eighth grades. I must have gotten to be pretty good, too, because people would say, "Hey, when you go to Rogers High School, you're going to play football, aren't you?" If you played on the community team and went on to become a high school stud, it was a big deal. College players didn't matter—nobody even thought about that. But if you could be the high school kingpin, life was good. Since I had some success playing, football became my favorite sport, but I really liked boxing. This was during the era of *Friday Night Fights* on television.

"When he was playing little league football, his coach told him he'd never be a football player. He'd never make it."

Fred Tiller

Sponsored by Gillette, they were always from Madison Square Garden. You could see the No. 1- or No. 2-ranked guy fight No. 3 or No. 4 just about every other week. You always saw the top fighters, from featherweight Willie Pepp to heavyweight champion Rocky Marciano. The middleweights seemed to be the most featured, though—fighters like Jake LaMotta, Gene Fullmer, Kid Gavilan, Carmen Basilio, and the great Sugar Ray Robinson.

I thought I wanted to be a boxer. We lived outside the city, so we didn't have access to the Police Athletic League. I remember one time, when I was still in grade school, we made a boxing ring in our yard. We had these oversized boxing gloves that you could hardly lift, let alone swing and hurt anybody. We'd spar a lot, just fooling around. But one day, I had this fight against a neighborhood kid. He hit me on the end of the nose and ... oh, God ... my eyes started watering. "I don't need any more of this," I said. I was a one-fight guy. In defense of my abbreviated career, he was two years older than me and substantially bigger—plus I think my manager overscheduled me.

My dad was a very introverted, silent, but strong person. He didn't say much, but he loved the fights. If I could sit still on the couch, I'd get to watch the fights with him, which was a very big deal to me.

I was born in our house on Collomore Road—a dead-end street on the west edge of Toledo, Ohio, near the intersection of Reynolds Road and Dorr Street. In fact, my youngest brother, Marv, was the only one of five kids who was born in a hospital. It was a very humble beginning. My folks actually borrowed the money from my grandparents to buy that house—a three-bedroom house that would hold five of us kids. And it's the only house they ever owned until after they retired.

My house was the last one on the right, and stayed the last one until a house was built at the very end of the street—taking our baseball field away from us. Although we were asked not to play there anymore, we continued to do so throughout the house's construction and even after it was finished, despite the owner's objections. When I hit a ball through a window in that new house, which cost three weeks' wages from my paper route, things got dicey.

Friends were scarce on that dead-end street, but my life changed when a kid named Larry Seegert moved in sometime around junior high. Although I went to Catholic school and he went to public school, he was the only guy on that street who was my age and would play catch at any hour. Later, we would play baseball together in high school. Larry, whom we called "Swampfire," didn't play football, though. He was a southpaw starter, and I was the centerfielder, but we'd played catch together for so long that I'd catch whenever he pitched.

Both of my parents are deceased. Dad died in August of 1982 at 74, and Mom died in July of 1999 at 86. I was actually named after my mother. I can remember my mother saying that my dad named me after her. My mother's name was Josephine, but everyone called her 'Jo.' Her maiden name was Bolz, and she was a German girl whose grandparents immigrated to America. My paternal grandmother's name was Zigler, which also is German, and her parents also immigrated to this country. Grandfather Tiller was English.

My dad's name was Francis, but he went by Fran, or Franny, among family members. He was a blue-collar worker. I don't know where he started work, but he finished with the DeVilbiss Company. He worked there for more than 30 years as a sheet-metal inspector. DeVilbiss did duct work for commercial heating and cooling jobs but was most famous for its compressors. He became very uncomfortable with his job in his later years because his superiors, in an effort to increase profits, oftentimes pressured him to approve materials that didn't meet the specs. He developed an ulcer and didn't really enjoy the last five or 10 years of his working life. He was so honest that it bothered him to know that a duct might be off even a fraction of an inch. But they'd say, "Fran, go ahead and put your stamp on it; and let's go." He lived in fear that the government was going to track him down and get him for fudging an eighth of an inch on a duct and throw him in jail.

Both my parents were extremely honest people. I found a five-dollar bill at the end of the street one time, and my mother made me go door to door and ask everybody in the neighborhood if they had lost a five-dollar bill—I must have been around 10 years old. Fortunately, no one said they did. I lived among honest neighbors. I can remember being with my mother at a store and she didn't think she was charged enough. She said, "I think I owe you 12 more cents," and she made the clerk total it up again.

Dad didn't graduate from high school, but I think he eventually got his GED. Mom graduated from Libby High School in Toledo. Since I didn't turn six until December—and there wasn't a state requirement on entering school at any particular age—I started at age five, which created a lasting impression since I was always younger than my classmates. Entering my senior year of high school, I was only 16. My parents sent me to school early because my mother was working the assembly line at Champion Spark Plugs. Although my brother, Marv, had just been born, she refused her maternity leave to make sure she'd keep her job.

My dad always taught me, "If you have an opportunity to keep your mouth shut, you should take advantage of it." However, I find that most of what I say on a repetitive basis comes from my mother. Occasionally, I find myself saying something, and don't know why—until I realize that she used to say the same thing.

Although both were pretty strict, my dad was by far the worst when it came to dishing out punishment. He was a fan of the iron fist, but he used a paddle. When you stepped out of line, you got your butt pad-

Standing in front of our house on Collomore Road with my dad and mom on my eighth-grade Confirmation Day. Photo provided by the Joe Tiller family

dled. I'm not sure whether he enjoyed that process, but it never seemed to bother him. That silent sternness probably made me closer to my mom, but he softened as soon as he became a grandfather (and then a great-grandfather).

I remember when I was in the seventh grade, though, and my dad got pretty excited. It was 1954, and a new Western Auto Hardware store had opened in town. For its grand opening, the store held a raffle, and my brother, Fred, won a refrigerator. They didn't want to give it to a kid, but there was no rule against it. Dad's grin stretched from ear to ear.

"I've never won anything in my life," he kept saying.

None of us had the heart to tell him, "Well, Pa … you didn't win this either—Fred won."

The family had never won anything, so damned if we didn't stop for dinner at Smuckers Restaurant, on Reynolds Road, about 10 blocks from our house. So far as I can remember, that's the first time I ate in a restaurant. That was kind of a red-letter day in my life. Pa was so excited that he also bought my brother a new bike, which probably cost 10 or 12 bucks.

My oldest brother, Chuck, and older sister, Janet, both went to vocational tech high schools—Chuck to Macomber High, Janet to Whitney High—which were adjacent all-male and all-female schools. Fred was the first of the siblings to go to college. He received some academic aid and graduated from the University of Toledo. Marv, the youngest, went to Montana State on a football scholarship, as I did. Chuck, who is five years older than I am, didn't necessarily influence me as a youngster other than he liked athletics. He played high school football, and I used to love to go to his games and learn who the players were. That's probably why I started playing football.

> "I was the oldest one, and I remember how Joe and Marv always used to tag along. Joe used to beg to play football with us. I always felt that's why he and Marv were better athletes—they had to be tougher to play against older kids. Joe didn't want to play with the little guys."
>
> Chuck Tiller

When I was a freshman, our township built a new high school, Rogers High. Janet was a member of the first class to graduate from Rogers, while I was in the first class to complete all four grades in the building. At Rogers, you had a choice between a vocational or a college-prep program. I was so in tune with vocational, that's what I chose. Coming from a blue-collar family, any encouragement we received at home regarding education was geared toward preparation for a skilled laborer's job. My family's philosophy was, "We're always going to have a roof over our heads, and we're always going to have food on the table." I never knew how much money my folks made. But I can remember a pay stub being left on the buffet—my dad's weekly pay stub. His take home was $59, and he had a family of five kids.

At Robert S. Rogers High School, there were 1,400 to 1,500 students in four grades. Of course, you knew nearly everyone in your class. We were fortunate enough to attract quality teachers since we were a new school in a new township. The majority of them were good educators and, more importantly, good people. We had an award-winning principal in Jack Fishbaugh, who first showed me how important leadership is to any organization. It was a very secure, nice place to go to school.

I didn't date much at first. I didn't have any money, so as a freshman, I wasn't interested in the dances. As a junior and senior, I went to all of them. I never really dated anybody regularly, though. No one ever had my class ring—I took pride in that. What a fool I was.

One of the reasons I didn't date much was because back then we didn't have multiple phones, we didn't have cell phones, and we didn't have portable phones. We had one phone connected to a wall jack that sat in the corner of our dining room. Everybody else in the house could hear your conversation. How the heck do you ask a girl out on a date when your whole family is sitting there listening to you?

I had to choose my sports wisely. I played football and baseball, but one of the more traumatic things in my life was getting cut from

My high school yearbook photol. Photo provided by the Joe Tiller family

the freshman basketball team. The grade school I attended didn't have a basketball team, so I was behind fundamentally. All the guys I had just played football with in the fall went out for basketball, and the better football players all made the basketball team, but I didn't. I knew it was going to be close, but I was hoping that I'd make the team since the head football coach was also the freshman basketball coach.

As a sophomore, I played football on the JV team again. I knew I wouldn't make the basketball team, so I just hung out as a gym rat. I just loved school—I never wanted to leave. I couldn't get enough of high school. I was an average student, but for four years, I never missed a day of high school. I wasn't a horrible student, but I wasn't a gifted student. I had to work for what I got—'Bs' were big in my life, 'As' were scarce. About the middle of my sophomore year, after taking wood shop, electricity classes, and the like, I decided, "This is not for me. I need to get out of this technical trade track and get on to a college-prep track."

I also made the JV baseball team as a sophomore and played baseball in the summer; but that also was about the time I decided I needed to spend more time with football. There was no weight training back then as we have today. You just conditioned during the summer. I worked very hard so I could start two-a-days in better shape than anyone. I would go on three-mile runs every single night. I just used to love that. They were almost masochistic-type workouts. I'd do push-ups and sit-ups, things like that, where you'd go until you couldn't go anymore. I used to go over on the side of the bleachers and put my head under the front-row seats and try to lift them up, or put a towel down and push down, trying to work on my neck muscles.

Duane Fender, the JV football coach, had played at Michigan State. He took a bunch of us players to a game at MSU every year. I went as a sophomore. It wasn't my first college game—I had snuck into some Toledo games—but this was something special. I was just awestruck. I thought, "Hey, this might be something I want to do. I might want to do this college thing."

Remember, this was a blue-collar family, and I was thinking about going college prep? At home, it was kind of like, "What do you do with that? What happens if you don't go to college? We don't have money to pay your way to college."

When, in December, I finally turned 16, I was a junior in high school and eligible for driver's education. I had a learner's permit allowing me to drive with a licensed driver over 18. My mom was great. We'd go someplace, and she'd say to Dad, "Don't you want Joe to drive? Don't you think it'd be a good experience for him to drive?"

I wanted to drive, but I wasn't real anxious to do it with him in the car. One day, however, Dad decided it was okay for me to drive. So I pulled out of our driveway on our dead-end street, and I started driving up the road. This kid was riding his bike along the side of the road, so I moved over and really slowed down. I couldn't have been going more than five or 10 miles per hour, but as I started to pass him, the kid turned into the right-front fender of the car, on the side where my dad was sitting. You'd have thought that I'd run that kid over in cold blood. … My dad was on me immediately.

"What's the matter with you? What the hell makes you think you can drive? You could kill somebody!"

I started shrinking in my seat. My mother, bless her heart, said, "Fran, will you just knock it off? The boy ran into the car—Joe didn't run into the boy."

She rescued me, but I tried never to drive again with him in the car.

My junior year was a breakout year for me—the first time that my life changed due to sports. During the football season, I played every minute of every game with the exception of one. I played all but about three minutes against the Bowling Green Bobcats in a game we won

36-0. I played offensive tackle, defensive tackle, and on all the kicking units, everything. I just loved it.

I think my coach pushed me for all-league because I played all the time. I knew I wasn't a bad player, but I didn't think I was that good of a player. But I made first-team all-league. The first I knew about it was when it came out in the paper. My coach never said anything. I noticed other people thought that was a big deal. Suddenly, my classmates wanted to know if I wanted to go to parties. I was becoming a big man on campus. That told me, "Hey, maybe this football is not a bad thing. Maybe there's more to this."

Following my junior year, I committed myself to doing whatever I had to do to go to college and continue playing football.

When I was younger, I'd sneak into University of Toledo games for entertainment. After my junior year, I'd sneak into a game to see what the guys were doing, how they were blocking and tackling. Maybe, in a way, that was the beginning of my coaching career, although that wasn't on my mind.

The game I probably remember most from my junior year was against those Bowling Green Bobcats. Although we beat them easily, they had a real tough guy named Tom Pendleton. Since we were cruising, I thought I was cruising, too. Then I ran into Tom Pendleton. On the first play of the game, I went to block him, and he blasted me into the backfield. I thought, "Man, oh, man, Tiller—you've got to crank it up. You're playing against your first real player." Most guys, the ball is snapped, they rise up and try to find the ball. This guy, he didn't care where the ball was—he was going to knock the snot out of anything that moved in front of him. Tom Pendleton made all-league, so when I made all-league, I knew I was in good company.

In my senior yea, I weighed a whopping 212 pounds, was elected co-captain, and I made all-league again. Back then, we only had a backfield coach and a line coach to work with the head coach. All the coaches were part of the faculty, unlike today's era, where many peo-

My senior year at Rogers High School—I thought I was a real tough guy (note the trail of blood on my left leg). Photo provided by the Joe Tiller family

ple can offer their time and expertise to local athletics. And as I reflect upon those days now, as a coach, I remember we did an awful lot of scrimmage work, and I suspect that was due to the lack of available coaches. During the games, your JV and frosh coaches helped out as spotters.

The last game of my high school career was against Clay. They were east side—we were west side. And they were very tough. Athletics were very important at that school, so Clay was the bar by which we measured ourselves. Before that game, we warmed up in a downpour. The rain let up before kickoff, but the field was very muddy—and I had to block a linebacker. Whenever I'd block linebackers, I'd dive at their feet, try to trip them up. All my life as a player, no one ever corrected me. Since the field was so slippery, I couldn't use that technique—I'd miss him. I had to try to run through the guy to be effective.

"I wish I had known this three years ago—*this* is how you block a linebacker."

In my last high school game, I finally learned how.

Sometimes games weren't as intense. I don't remember the team now, but we were giving them a sound beating. Now, I didn't really place kick, but I was a decent kicker—decent like "emergency" kicker. The coaches always thought I was joking when I told them I could kick, but once they saw me fooling around in practice my junior year, nailing several consecutive extra points, my coach was like, "Okay, Joe, I want you to be the backup kicker." Since our kicker was doing a good job, I went through most of my senior year without having ever kicked an extra point. Yet, we were way ahead of this team so my coach told me, "Joe, go ahead and kick off for us."

"Kick off? I've never kicked off," I thought to myself. "I've never practiced kicking off. That was just a favor, his making me the backup kicker for two years. … Oh, God! I've got to kick off."

Normally I wore glasses, but not when I played football. You don't have to see very far as a lineman. However, as I was preparing to kick off and run downfield, I was thinking, "I hope I can see that ball as I get closer to it. … Whatever you do, don't look up." You learn that last tidbit kicking extra points—you were in trouble if you looked up. When the ref blew the whistle, Tiller started charging. I had no idea where the ball went, of course, because I had to keep my head down just to kick the ball in the first place. I was sprinting blind until, maybe 10 yards downfield, the ball suddenly landed right in front of me.

I must have kicked the thing 30 yards high and 10 yards long. That was the end of my kicking career.

Chapter 2

MONTANA STATE

Coming out of high school in the 1960s was much different than today. Recruiting didn't begin until after the football season was complete. Then your high school coaches would send out your 16-millimeter film. Hopefully, college coaches would come by to watch the film or, if they'd already seen the film, to talk to you. No national letters of intent existed—although there were conference letters, which eliminated you from attending another school within the conference, but didn't protect against the student pursuing colleges outside the conference.

No one was in a hurry since scholarships weren't passed out until March, April, or even May. I don't know anyone who was recruited early in my school days. No one was recruited as an underclassman, and no one had a scholarship until after his senior season. Perhaps you'd receive letters from colleges during your final season, but they were very general, and no promises were made. Yet, it was still fun to see who sent you letters.

As it turned out, I simply wasn't big enough, at 6-foot-1 and 212 pounds, to merit any interest from any Big Ten Conference teams, and trips to those schools were purely unofficial. I wanted the Big Ten to show interest in me, of course, but I never got anything from them. The Mid-American Conference schools, though, were interested. I visited both Miami of Ohio and Oxford, and liked them both. I really didn't want to go to the University of Toledo, which was on Bancroft Street. We used to call it Bancroft High—when you're a local kid, it's not very sexy to go to the hometown college. It's as if you never went anywhere. Bowling Green, coached by the legendary Doyt Perry, was really good at that time, and together that had me interested. They had me there on a trip but didn't offer at that time since they were waiting on a couple of other guys. But they reneged on a scholarship after I'd made the trip. I'm not sure that I would have gone there anyway, it being just 23 miles from Toledo. I looked at Western Michigan, Kent State, and Ohio University, but once I knew that the Big Ten schools didn't want me, I kind of eliminated the MAC, too.

There were no limits on recruiting visits back then; you could take as many as you wanted. I was set to visit New Mexico, but Marv Levy left for a coaching job at California, and their recruiting came to a temporary halt. A guy from Ohio named Joe Berry, a teammate of my high school coach at the University of Toledo, was an assistant coach at Montana State, and he used to come back to Ohio to recruit. Montana State was recruiting me, but then Berry took a job at Idaho. After he left Montana State, coach Tom Parac took over my recruitment, and a panic reaction near the end of the recruiting season finally prompted me to sign with Montana State.

Recruiting was foreign to my parents, but they did know that a scholarship meant they didn't have to pay for school. I grew up in a lower-middle class Midwest family. My parents both lived through the Depression, so they fought to find work. There always was a premium placed on having a job. "Get a job, son. Make sure that whatever work you choose, there will always be a need for it in this country, so you can stay employed." Stay employed. Stay employed. That's what was hammered home in my house. They really didn't care if I went to the University of Toledo or the University of Tokyo, so long as somebody else paid for my schooling. They didn't have any money. My oldest brother and my sister didn't go to college. Fred went to Toledo and lived at home all four years. He got a bunch of academic aid. Because he got good grades in college, and he kept his aid, I'd be shocked if my parents paid more than $300 for his education. My parents knew that I didn't have Fred's academic prowess, and they were aware that schools gave athletic scholarships—but that's about all they knew, since neither of them were ever part of a college environment. They never once said, "Hey, it'd be nice if you were going to school here close to home where we could see you play." They didn't care—they just wanted someone to pay for their kid's education. That was the bottom line.

Once I had signed with Montana State, I tried to tell my dad that the letter of intent was just for that conference. "No, you gave that man your word," he told me. "You said you're going to school there, and that's where you're going to school." If that hadn't happened, I might have taken another trip or two. But I was told the decision had been made. As I said, my dad was the silent type, he never said too much, but he got excited when Montana State started recruiting me, and I don't know why. Maybe as a youth he wanted to go out West or something.

One evening my dad asked me what I was going to do with this college stuff. I told him that I really didn't know. He said, "Well, I'm not you, but if I had a chance to go out there to that beautiful country of Montana, that's where I think I'd go."

Since I'd never visited, it seemed exotic, with the mountains and all. My dad hinted that he thought it was a good deal, too. At that time, though, I would have flunked geography—I thought Montana was near Oklahoma.

So my dad asked me, "What are you going to study?"

"I think I'll study to be a teacher," I told him. When he asked why, I answered, "Well, teachers are always employed, and they get two months off in the summer. That sounds like a pretty good lifestyle to me."

As it turned out, my Montana State scholarship may have been the only thing that got my folks to visit the West. They weren't much for traveling, but they really liked their trips to Montana.

———

At freshman orientation, the provost, or some other college official, welcomed us to Montana State *College*. Originally, Montana State College was in Bozeman, and Montana State University was in Missoula. Later, the names were changed to Montana State University in Bozeman and the University of Montana in Missoula.

As I sat at the orientation waiting to take the placement tests, the speaker was telling us how important they were. And then he said, "Look to your left and look to your right, because four years from now, the probability is that neither of those two people will be here." I said to myself, "I'm going to be here. I don't know about these people sitting next to me, but I'm going to be here."

I roomed with Don Wheeler—a high school teammate and running back who was also on scholarship—making the transition much easier. On the first day of classes, I went into the dormitory dining hall. Students were throwing their books on top of a coat rack and hanging their coats on the hooks. All I could think as I saw that was, "You don't do that in Toledo, Ohio—when I come back those books and my coat will be gone."

I got into line with my books in one hand, my tray in the other. A lady looked at me peculiarly and said, "Hey, son, aren't you going to take your coat off?"

"Yeah, when I get over to my chair," I told her.

Here I am as a junior at Montana State, when we were still referred to as Montana State College (note the MSC letters on the socks). Photo provided courtesy of Montana State University

"Well, they've got shelves out there," she said.

"I ain't putting my books out there," I told her. I did that for about three days before I finally started putting my books and my coat on those shelves like everybody else. You know, I never did lose a thing during all the time I was there. I always liked that about the West, and I developed the impression that more honest people live in the West and in small towns. I was becoming a Westerner at heart, although I didn't know it at the time.

At our first team meeting, our coach, George Marinkovich, said, "Okay, guys, we're just going to have a little conditioning test here to see what kind of shape we're in." He introduced us to some guy he said was going to lead us around the track and bring us in on time for a six-minute mile. Well, I'm thinking, "Six minutes, that's a long time." But on the other side of the coin, I'd never in my life timed myself running a mile. And we were at 4,800 feet elevation, so the air was a little thinner. I didn't know that we were going to be tested— we weren't forewarned.

I found out later that this leader was a cross-country runner and a miler on the track team. During a big publicity stunt, he raced a quarter horse for a quarter of a mile—and he beat the horse. This cat could run. For the first lap, I kept him in sight. The second lap, he got a little bit farther ahead. The third lap, I couldn't see him. And I could barely finish the fourth lap. I was totally out of gas. I thought to myself, "Am I really in that bad of shape?" I was really discouraged and depressed. I didn't make the time limit, but there was no penalty. It sure was a humbling experience, and I was thinking, "Am I ever going to be able to play football here?"

I had been very fortunate in that all of the time I had played sports, I had never gotten hurt. But then, maybe in the second or third game for the freshman team, I made a tackle and ended up on my back. One of my teammates landed on top of me, and I broke my right wrist. It was very severe—a big-time break. I came off the field and told the trainer, and he told me to spread my fingers apart so he

This is the cover of the 1963 Montana State football media guide.
Photo provided courtesy of Montana State University

could tape it. I went back on the field for another play or two, but I had to come out to have the tape cut off because my hand had swollen so much that the skin had puffed through the tape. The trainer saw that and said I was done for the day. After I got X-rayed, they called my parents, and I had surgery that night.

The doctors told me that I had to decide if I wanted to keep playing football. They told me if I ever broke that wrist again it would be immobilized. I couldn't believe they would suggest that I should consider giving up football. That never crossed my mind. In response to their warnings about my wrist, I thought, "Well, that's not that big of a price to pay for playing football." What the hell ... I was 17 years old, so I never even considered that.

They operated in October and put me in a cast that went up to my biceps. I had a horrible time and got sick after the surgery. I remember lying on my back in the hospital, waking up with my arm tied in place. I reached up and broke the gauze holding my arm up so I could roll over. Because I was sick, I wanted to be on my side, just in case I vomited.

It was not easy going to college and trying to take notes in class with a cast on your wrist. Just trying to hold a pencil was an ordeal. But that wasn't the biggest challenge I faced—that was trying to wipe my butt. I'll never forget the first time I went to the bathroom, and I couldn't get my right hand back there, so I put the toilet paper in my left hand. The problem was, I couldn't find my butt with my left hand. I was wiping my cheeks and struggling big time. To this day, though, I consider myself ambidextrous when it comes to going to the bathroom.

Being 1,600 miles from home and not being able to play the sport I'd played all my life, I became very lonely and very introverted. I wasn't very happy. I didn't do very well academically, and I was homesick. I thought everything in Montana was backward and slow. They only played rock-and-roll music for one hour a night on the local radio station. Otherwise, it was that country stuff. It was called "Country and

Western" back then, and I couldn't stand it. It was hillbilly music. Everybody who sang it had a twang, and I just couldn't relate to it. (Since then, I've come full circle—today, I probably own about 200 country CDs.)

Unhappy and unable to play football, I began to question whether I wanted to stay at Montana State. Actually, I began to question whether I wanted to stay in college, period. Fortunately, I had two people who took a personal interest in my progress. One was a wonderful English composition instructor named Dr. Titus Kurtichanov. In my first quarter (we were on a quarter system instead of semesters), I think I got two Cs and two Ds. I didn't flunk out of school, but I was close. I struggled with my writing, and Dr. Kurtichanov helped me improve my skills. He also learned who everyone was in his class. He knew I was Joe from Toledo, and that was encouraging to me. Dr. Kurtichanov gave me the confidence to do college work.

The other person who most influenced me was Dr. Alton Oviatt, who was an excellent lecturer in world history—which I didn't like, but he made it interesting. He also took an interest in his students, and he knew my first name. Dr. Oviatt actually got me to thinking about possibly majoring in history. Those two guys gave me a reason to go back to Montana State. If not for them, I often wonder if I ever would have earned a college degree. A third person who helped me make it through that first year was Ed Hanson. He and his wife, Laura, were the dorm proctors where I lived, and he provided encouragement away from the classroom. We remain friends to this day.

When I went home for Christmas, I was still wearing that cast. They eventually cut it down some, but I wore that cast until May. Going back home for the first time, I wanted to take a lot of clothes because, seeing all your high school classmates going to the Christmas or New Year's Eve parties, I wanted to look sharp. I didn't own a suitcase, but my parents had bought me a metal footlocker, and that's what I took to college with me. Everything I owned fit in that one footlocker. For my trip home at Christmas, I packed damn near everything I had back into that footlocker and traveled by train back to Toledo. I had to change trains in Chicago, and I had to drag that heavy metal footlocker through the train station. What a pain in the butt that was. ... I was just hoping the strap didn't break off.

During the Christmas break, I had decided I really wanted to transfer schools. I wanted to get back into the league I had shunned—the MAC. I was ready to go to Miami, to Toledo, to Bowling Green, to Kent State, to anybody that would have me. But it's hard to walk into a football office with a cast on, tell them you're interested in transferring, and expect them to give you some money. And if I didn't get a scholarship to transfer, I was out of business. So after being rejected by the schools that recruited me earlier, I went back to Montana State. My dad told me, "If you're not going to college, then you're going into the service." That motivated me to go back and study a little harder.

I really don't remember the winter, except that I made it through the winter quarter and did a little better academically. Finally, spring arrived and they let me practice with a cast on. That was good for me. I started meeting some of the varsity guys, and in the spring of 1961, I made another trip back to Ohio with the infamous Jerry "Firehead" Johnson driving, Dan "The Pardner" Greer in the middle-front seat, and "Slick" Jack Cameron, who had a duck-tail haircut, riding shotgun. Jerry was a running back-defensive back from Cuyahoga Falls, Ohio; Dan was a tight end-defensive end from Columbus, Ohio; and Jack was a running back-defensive back from Allentown, Pennsylvania. Don Wheeler and I were in the back with some other guy. I never knew what those upperclassmen in the front seat did, but I knew that we rookies gave them 20 bucks—so the three of us probably paid for the whole trip. We drove non-stop with the six of us packed in that car.

We got all the way to Livingston, Montana, 26 miles away, and "The Pardner" Greer, who was probably in his mid-20s because he went into the Navy out of high school, said, "I'm getting tired of looking at your ugly faces." Tired of looking at us? We had 1,574 miles to go.

Greer then said, "Let's play a spelling game." And the other two guys up front just bust out laughing. The three of us in the back seat didn't know that Dan Greer is perhaps the world's worst speller—and he wanted to play a spelling game. The game is like Scrabble. You start out with a letter, and you have to keep adding to it. The word had to be four or more letters. And if you didn't think a guy could spell a word, you could challenge him. It took us all the way to Billings, 140 miles away, to get the rules down. Finally, we were ready to start playing the game.

So Jerry, a bright guy who majored in engineering, looks at "The Pardner" and said "Z." So Greer said, "You trying to stump me right off the bat? You sure you don't want to change to some other letter?" We drove a while, and Jack said, "Dan, this is your game, but isn't there some type of time limit? We're damn near to Minneapolis, and he still hasn't added the second letter."

Greer finally looked over at Jack and said, "B." Cameron, who's a business major, thinks for a minute and said, "I don't know. … I can't think of a word that starts out Z-B." Jerry looked over at Jack and said, "Challenge him. There isn't any word that begins with Z-B." Jack agreed, and said, "I challenge you." Greer crossed his arms, puffed up his chest, and said, "Zebra: Z-B-R-A."

Whenever we get together, the Zebra story will be told.

During my time in Bozeman, I became very good friends with Dan. I was out one night with "The Pardner," and we were doing what college guys do—drinking beer, laughing, telling jokes, and chasing skirts. It was during the summer, and Greer decided he wanted to make a run to Idaho Falls to see his girlfriend, the "Idaho Spud." He had a Model-T Ford, with a cut-off roof. He didn't have a second seat in the back, so he had put a rocking chair back there.

We were getting ready to head out, but he had a flat tire. So Dan said, "They have a Model-T over at the SAE house. Let's go over there and steal a tire off it." I had a little buzz, so I said, "Okay, if that's what you want to do." Well, we didn't have a jack, so I waited until he got everything loose, and I lifted up the front end of the car. It really wasn't that heavy, but he makes it sound like I lifted that car head high. We put his flat tire on their car, took their tire, and away we went.

When we arrived at West Yellowstone, we were tired as hell, so we decided to stay overnight in a city park. I'm from Ohio. I didn't know anything about grizzly bears, but I knew grizzly bears lived in Yellowstone National Park. Dan had a couple of sleeping bags in his car, but, hell, I'm thinking the bears are going to come and eat me alive. So, I put the sleeping bag underneath the Model-T, and that's where I slept.

The Model-T's radiator had been boiling over. We didn't have any water, but we had a 24-pack—maybe two—of Grain Belt beer. When I woke up in the morning, Dan was still sleeping. I checked the radiator—no water. So I started popping open those cans of Grain Belt and pouring the beer into the radiator. I figured we had to have some fluid in there.

And then Greer woke up and started yelling, "What are you doing? You're crazy, man!" But away we

"Joe and I used to work on campus during the summer patching roofs. We got this one job at Romney Gym–the old basketball gym with a round roof building. It had leaks, so Joe and I had to go up there and patch it.

"We got up on the roof, and Joe said, 'I'm not getting down on the side of that.' I had a rope, so I said, 'I'll go down and patch it. You hold on to the rope, in case I slip.' It was about three stories high. I told Joe to tie the rope around his waste. He said, 'Don't worry about it, I can handle it.' I went down the side; and I slipped and fell, almost bouncing over the gutter. One leg was over the side. I'm looking at Joe, yelling, 'Don't let go, don't let go.' But he pulled me right back up. From that point on, I made sure he tied the rope around himself, because if I went, he was going with me."

Dan "The Pardner" Greer

went to Idaho Falls. The beer worked. We made it there to visit his "Spud."

After a few hours, it was time to go back. We were driving through the canyon, from Yellowstone to Bozeman. Dan was up front driving, with his goofy-looking cowboy hat. I had a cowboy hat on too, and I was sitting in that rocking chair. It was kind of chilly, so I had grabbed a sleeping bag and put it on over my shoulders. When we were driving through the canyon, one of the guys we worked with drove by, recognized Dan, and honked.

The next day, back in Bozeman, that guy said, "Hey, Dan, I saw you driving up the canyon yesterday. Who was that big Indian sitting in the back seat?"

Chapter 3

FINDING EMPLOYMENT

Following my freshman year, I went back home for the last summer I'd spend in Toledo. An uncle, who was a superintendent with the roofers' union and had arranged for me to get a job the previous summer, had lined up some more work for me. The summer before I left for college, one of my summer jobs was unloading rolls of asphalt paper from a flatbed semi. A guy on the truck would put a roll on each of my shoulders, and I would lug them to the warehouse and unload them. It seemed like there were a thousand of them. When I got home that night, I thought the sides of my neck were on fire. That asphalt had worked its way into my skin, and it immediately blistered. Mom worked for a doctor, who sent some medicine home with her, but it took two weeks to heal.

Between my freshman and sophomore years in college, I was part of a roofing crew that worked on a Ford plant in Monroe, Michigan. It was such a huge project that we only got one section done before it was time to return to college. Because of the summer heat, we were on the roof by 6:00 in the morning, and we'd quit at 2:30 in the afternoon. It was at least a 30-minute drive from Toledo to Monroe, and I had to get up at 4:30 in the morning to catch my ride. I didn't have a car, so I would stand out on the highway and wait for one of the guys to pick me up, and I gave him three dollars a week for gas money. As it turned out, roofing was a great experience because it motivated me to get a college degree. It was a good life lesson. At the end of that summer, I knew I was going to see this college thing through.

When I went back to Montana State for my sophomore year, I wasn't a starter on the football team, but I got to play a lot—and I began to like football again. We didn't have a weightlifting program, but we did isometrics and isotonic stuff. I never thought too much about it, but luckily I stumbled into a small weight room. After buying a weightlifting magazine, I started getting into it. I enjoyed it because I could feel myself getting stronger. As a result of the weightlifting and having a good spring practice, I was in position to be a starter as a junior.

I never went on a spring break. I instead took advantage of the opportunity to work on campus. The field house at Montana State—where they once held the middleweight world championship fight between Gene Fullmer and Joey Giardello—was a round building, similar to Purdue's Mackey Arena. It was a multipurpose building with a dirt floor. They even staged indoor rodeos there. If you stayed on campus during spring break, you could make some extra money helping to remove the portable basketball floor. I didn't have much money besides my football scholarship, which included room, board, books, tuition and 15 dollars a month incidentals. I had to work for those 15 dollars, which was big money. They usually paid two dollars an hour, so you had to put in around eight hours a month.

The freshman athletes usually had to clean the stadium on Saturdays, or stay after basketball games to sweep out the field house. One of my jobs that first year was digging fencepost holes by hand. Upperclassmen got better jobs, such as sweeping the basketball court at halftime or working the concession stands, so when the game was over you could go home. Between my junior and senior years, I worked in the service shop on campus. That summer they were going to put a new roof on Lewis and Clark Hall, which was a three- or four-story dormitory. They wanted to know if anybody had any roofing experience, which, of course, I did. One of the real prestige assignments—if you can call it that—on a roofing crew was to be the kettle operator. He was the guy down below who worked that big black kettle on two wheels that had the roaring fire and that bubbling, hot tar, and that spigot to draw out the boiling tar.

So guess what? Who ended up being the kettle operator? Ol' Joe T. himself.

As a junior, I had some success playing football as a two-way starter. At that time, college football was experimenting with cost-saving ideas, one of which was platoon football. We had a pretty good team. During one game I got credit for blocking a field goal, and we won. My line coach, Jim Sweeney, was ecstatic. His wife was pregnant, and they were due to have a baby any day. That night, Sweeney went home, and he was so excited that he told his wife they were going to name their son Joseph. She shot back, "The hell with him, he can have his own kids. This kid is going to be named Daniel."

Sweeney took over as the head coach for my senior season, when I was a co-captain and started once again. I missed a couple games with an ankle injury, so I was second-team all-conference instead of first team. Still, I had a pretty good season. We played Tulsa and Utah State, which were big games for Montana State. The Tulsa and Utah State players voted me to their all-opponent teams. I was

"Joe was my first captain and probably the most coachable player I ever had. He was a very intelligent, disciplined guy who had a quiet leadership about him. He was one of the few linemen that I've coached who had an overall view of the big picture.

"When I lost him at Washington State, I might as well have given up the ghost, because he was the backbone of the program. I've always said that Joe was the best coach I've ever had.

"Joe was a no-nonsense guy back then. I don't ever remember him even trying to be a comedian. He was not a fun guy. His fun was being able to see his players execute. They had total confidence in what they were doing because of his teaching techniques. I never, ever saw any kind of frivolity. I think they had a good time, but it was in knowing that they could kick ass."

Jim Sweeney

35

the only I-AA player on either of their all-opponent teams.

As a young head coach, Sweeney was a stickler for details. He would have the coaches teach one another on their respective positions; and, as a result, you learned a lot of football in those days. Whenever anyone went to a clinic, you were expected to return with notes and coach up the staff! He had a passion for the game like no one I've ever known. He taught toughness first and foremost. (He was the son of a Butte, Montana, hard-rock miner—I never knew that rocks had different degrees of hardness, but he always referred to his dad as a 'hard-rock miner.') He was a "hard-rock" coach!

> "I'll never forget the Montana-Montana State game during Joe's senior year. Joe was a two-way tackle. He just kicked ass in that game. On offense, he was knocking people all over the place, and on defense, he was all over the field. If I ever had a proudest moment about Joe, it was at that game.
>
> "About the middle of the fourth quarter, Montana State was ahead enough that Coach Sweeney—I think he did it on purpose—took Joe out of the game early, and the people in the stands stood up, started clapping and yelling his name, 'TILLER, TILLER, TILLER.' That usually happens to backs, not linemen.
>
> "I was like, 'Jesus Christ, this is my brother.' I went back to my dorm room and wrote my mom and dad a letter—it was at least five pages long. I told them about the whole game because I was so proud of what he did."
>
> Marv Tiller

Coach Sweeney was a bulldog as well, a former Golden Gloves fighter with huge fists. He was a tough, aggressive, gregarious Irishman. He single-handedly got me invited to play in the East-West Shrine game, which was unheard of for a player from a small school such as Montana State. When I got back from the game, a Shriners group in Great Falls, Montana, wanted Coach Sweeney and me to attend one of their luncheons. So Coach and his wife took me from Bozeman to Great Falls, stopping at a bar in Winston, Montana, so he could buy a pack of cigarettes.

We were wearing coats and ties, which caught the attention of two cowboys sitting at the bar. One of them turned around and said, "Look at these tootie-fruities with their ties on."

Sweeney quickly responded with, "You got a problem with that?"

The cowboy swung around off the bar stool, stood up, and said, "Yeah, I got a problem with that."

Suddenly, Sweeney said, "Well, how about this?" And—boom—he hit that cowboy with a punch that knocked him to the floor.

Man, I jumped back, not believing what I had just witnessed. As a player, I knew you didn't want to cross Coach Sweeney, but now I was really convinced that *nobody* wanted to cross him. Then Jim straightened his tie and said to the other cowboy, "You want any of this?" Nervously, the cowboy said, "Nope."

Jim got his cigarettes, and we went back to the car. I was sitting in the back seat, waiting for him to say something to his wife, but he didn't say a word. I sat motionless for the next 100 miles, because I didn't want him to reach back and backhand me if I would have said, "Hey, why don't you tell her what happened in there?" I was like a little kid—I wasn't about to squeal on the old man.

Academics became more fun my senior year, kind of like high school all over again. Socially, I was interacting more with people, just because I was more confident. I finally settled on a major and decided I was going to be a teacher. I majored in social science because that would allow me to teach government, world history, American history, sociology, psychology, or geography. My degree is a B.S. in secondary education, with an emphasis on social science. My minors were physical education and history, but my favorite subjects were philosophy and psychology.

I never missed a day of class in high school, and I went three and a half years at Montana State without skipping class. Because of the pro football draft, though, I missed some classes during the spring of my senior year. I got drafted by the then-Boston Patriots of the American Football League and was placed on the negotiation list of the Calgary Stampeders of the Canadian Football League as well. No NFL team drafted me, but the Pittsburgh Steelers offered me a contract.

After some negotiating, I signed with Calgary for a $1,500 signing bonus. With some money in my pocket, I decided to skip some classes—I figured that I didn't need college anymore. I was going to be a pro player for the rest of my life. I got an F in geography, and I think I failed history, too.

I got cut by Calgary and then went to Montreal and got cut again. I didn't really understand the inner workings of the CFL. It's not so much about making the team as it is trying to compete with the other "imports"—a limited number of American players on each team. There were 32 players on the team, 17 non-imports (Canadians) and 15 imports. If a team needed an imported defensive back more than an imported defensive lineman, I was in trouble. The final preseason game was probably my best one, and I thought I had it made. But a couple days later, I got the infamous call from the coach, wanting to see me in his office, "… and by the way, bring your playbook." I got cut.

Football in the CFL is a summer sport, so I went back to school in the fall, did my student teaching during the winter quarter, and got my degree in March 1965. Coach Sweeney wanted someone to help coach the freshman line. They didn't have enough money to hire me, but they had enough money to put me back on scholarship. I was most thankful because that allowed me to finish my schooling. I began coaching that fall and continued to coach at Montana State until 1971. I felt very fortunate to begin my coaching career at the collegiate level at the tender age of 22.

It wasn't until my second year of coaching that Coach Sweeney began to treat me like a coach instead of a player. But I had to threaten to quit before things changed. There was no daylight speed limit on the interstates in Montana, but there was a 55 miles-per-hour limit at night. Jim couldn't drive 55—he couldn't bear the thought of driving 55. He was one point away from losing his license when he received a speeding ticket and had to go to court. If he said anything, the judge was going to drop the hammer, so Coach had to take it. That judge just proceeded to rip a strip off him. No one, at that time in his life, had ever treated Jim like that, so when he returned to the office he was not in a good mood. In fact, he was steaming, and he proceeded to jump all over me.

I looked at him and said, "You're nuts—to hell with you. Take this job and stick it where the sun don't shine." I quit. I got up, walked out of the office, went down to the Safeway store, got a bunch of empty boxes out of the Dumpster in the back, came back, and started packing my stuff.

"What are you doing?" Jim asked me.

"I don't have to talk to you," I told him. "I'm out of here."

I loaded up all my stuff and left. I was ready to find another job. I'd had enough of this guy.

Gene Bourdet, the athletic director, called me at home and said, "Joe, you really need to rethink this."

I explained how Jim was treating me like one of his players. "Somebody screws up around there, and I'm the guy that catches hell," I said. "I'm sick and tired of it. I don't need it." The three of us had a meeting, and Coach Sweeney agreed that he was treating me like a player. From that day on, our relationship changed. I became Coach Tiller; I had more responsibility; and my contributions were recognized. I felt as if I finally had become a coach.

When you first start out in the coaching profession, you coach the way you were coached. I coached the way Jim had coached me—a very hard-nosed, intensely disciplined style of coaching. My guys responded to that type of coaching, which is pretty typical of offensive linemen. They're not the out-front guys who are looking for the publicity. They're blue-collar, lunch-bucket guys. That fit right in line with my style of coaching. The most important thing I learned from Coach Sweeney was tough love.

Sweeney left Montana State in 1969 to become the head coach at Washington State, and he didn't invite me to go along—I guess that's the graceful way to say it. And I don't know why. I never asked, and I was never given an explanation. Instead, he rehired Sonny Holland, who had coached for him at Montana State as his line coach but had quit.

Tiller: Not Your Average Joe

"I played at Washington State, for Jim Sweeney from 1969 through 1972. Joe joined us for my junior year, to coach the defensive line. I was an offensive lineman, but we would watch what was going on. We all thought he was 60 years old but he wasn't even 30 yet. He wore thick, black glasses and had big, strong legs. He never smiled and was as tough as they came. I mean TOUGH.

"He used to have the defensive linemen hang towels off the chin-up bars and made them grab those towels to do their pull-ups because it would strengthen their forearms for the pass rush. We'd be in the locker room after practice, and those defensive linemen would come in looking like they'd gone through the Bataan Death March. We'd tell them, 'Better you than me, having to put up with that guy.'

"As fate would have it, in the spring of 1972, Sweeney moved Tiller over to offense, so the defensive guys got the last laugh. We were all nervous and uptight because now we were going to get it.

"I was the only senior in the offensive line, and I can remember spring ball that year like it was yesterday. The first practice wasn't that bad, so we went into the locker room and told the defensive guys, 'That was a piece of cake.' The second day, we weren't as focused as we should've been. We were all huddled around Tiller, when one of our second- or third-string tackles was watching some girls walk by or something, and Tiller took a football, threw it, and hit him in the helmet. All of us came to attention immediately.

"Tiller said, 'I'm going to tell you something right now, and it's something I don't want you to forget. This is going to be the best offensive front in the Pac-8, and there's two ways we can get there—either you're going to get tough on yourselves, or I'm going to have to make you tough. And I guarantee you, if I have to make you tough, half of you are going to quit. Now let's get to work.'

"And then we went to work. Oh, my God! He was a perfectionist, and we were a bunch of misfits. We went to boot camp, and every practice was pure hell. He had these pipes made with 2-x-8 planks. For the first 30 minutes of practice, we would be down going through what he called 'the chutes.' If you stood up, you'd break your neck. We were always down in the power position hitting each other. It was a torture cell.

"Then we'd go through a series of five-minute drills, and if it wasn't done to perfection, when the period was over, he'd say, 'We'll repeat this drill after practice.' There wasn't any 20-hour rule in those days. A practice could go three hours and many times did. We'd scrimmage some at the end of most practices, then we'd run our wind sprints, and then go in and lift weights. And Tiller's guys would have to put the pads back on, go back out on the field, and repeat those drills.

"One time during fall camp, about the fifth day, we repeated so many drills that the rest of the team had gone to training table for lunch and were coming back to go over to the dorm, and we were still out there. Sometimes we'd go an extra hour repeating drills.

"Joe was a perfectionist and keen on discipline. There was no nonsense. He picked his five guys, and we played virtually every down for 11 games—all at new positions. Of those five guys, three of them were first-team all-conference, one was two-time all-conference and the other was three-time all-conference. Mentally, we were convinced we were the toughest bunch. We were better schooled, better trained and in excellent condition.

"We had the utmost respect for him, but we were scared of him. When we would watch film with him, he'd be chewing on his wrist, like an animal trying to get out of a trap. But he was a great teacher; it wasn't all negative.

"Much of who and what I am today, I wouldn't be without Joe Tiller's influence on my life. He made me realize how far I could push myself and what I had to do to realize my potential. He made me accountable and he put me in a leadership position. He made a man out of me.

"It doesn't surprise me a bit that he's had the success he's had."

Bill Moos

Tom Parac, a graduate of Montana State and a longtime assistant there, was named the head coach, and he kept me on his staff, giving me a lot of latitude and a $2,000 raise. We'd been a Winged-T team, but we wanted to look at some option and veer football, so I went to the University of Houston to study their offense, which we installed. My coaching colleague on offense was Sonny Lubick, a very good coach who later became the head coach at Montana State and then at Colorado State. My good fortune didn't last long. In 1971, Parac was named the athletic director, and he decided to bring back Sonny Holland, who was a legendary player at Montana State, as the head coach.

Again, I was not retained.

It was now early spring—after all the coaching jobs had changed hands. I had to start scrambling. I was married with a two-year-old daughter, and my wife, Arnette, was expecting our second child. She was a beautician, and she worked right up until she had the baby. She was supporting us while I was unemployed, perhaps the darkest time of my career.

We decided I should go to grad school and begin to pursue what I thought I wanted to do anyway, which was coach high school football and be a guidance counselor. So I went to Montana State that spring quarter and worked as a bouncer at a bar, the Corner Club, two nights a week for 10 dollars a night, while I tried to find a real job.

Finally, I accepted an assistant coaching job in Barberton, Ohio. It was a good-paying job, more than $10,000—which was about $2,000 more than I was making as a college assistant. I didn't think that was all that bad, since I had started my career making $5,500 a year on a 10-month contract, pumped gas at the Little Chief gas station, and did fitness training for the Peace Corps for $500 to live on the other two months.

After picking up a U-Haul rental trailer, I was back at the house packing when Coach Sweeney called. One of his coaches had quit to go into private business, and he wanted me to go to Washington State to coach the defensive line. Coach Sweeney didn't really interview me; he just offered me the job—and he wanted me to report immediately. I returned the U-Haul trailer and went to Washington State to work for my former coach for about $11,000. The next year, the offensive line coach left, and I took over that position. We were running the split-back veer, and because I had gone to Houston and had been running that offense, Coach Sweeney named me the offensive coordinator.

Then the Calgary Stampeders called. Their director of player personnel had come through Washington State looking for Canadian players, and we had a couple on our roster. I must have done something to impress him, because he recommended me to the coach at Calgary. Things were starting to happen for me. Vince Gibson at Kansas State had offered me a job, but Coach Sweeney talked me into staying. Jim had a chance to get in on the Arizona job, which I was hoping he would pursue, and New Mexico also wanted him. That winter, he actually had the Colorado job for 24 hours, but then the money guys decided they didn't want to bring in a coach with a losing record, so they hired Bill Mallory from Miami of Ohio.

After spending three years at WSU, I was convinced that we would never go to the Rose Bowl. Twenty-five years later, Mike Price and his great staff proved me wrong by going to Pasadena not once, but twice. I still believe that it was one of the greatest coaching jobs ever when the Cougars went to the Rose Bowl in 2001. Talk about doing more with less—no one's done better.

Nonetheless, in 1974, I wanted out of Washington State. After being there three years, I could see how hard it was to be successful at that time in Pullman. After I got that call from Calgary, I went up there to look around, liked what I saw, came back, and told Coach Sweeney, "I'm going to Calgary."

Chapter 4

O CANADA

When I told Coach Sweeney that I was going to leave, he thought it was a mistake. He thought we had our best team ever coming back, and we were going to the Rose Bowl.

But he thought that every year. At the end of training camp every season, we had the rookies put on a show. That year, one particular free-spirited freshman did an imitation of Coach Sweeney. He was up on the stage—with the whistle, the hat, the coaching shorts, the whole bit. He was pretending to be Coach Sweeney addressing the team, and he said, "And men, we go to the Rose Bowl once every 37 years, whether we want to or not; and this is our year."

Many guys laughed, but Coach Sweeney took great offense to that. However, sure enough, when I told him I was leaving, he said, "This is the year we go to the Rose Bowl."

We were maxed out at Washington State at that time. Although I liked the city of Pullman and the area, the program was really behind the other schools in what then was the Pacific-8 Conference. It was a challenging job. During my short stay in Canada as a player, I really liked Calgary. It was a lot like Denver, sitting next to the mountains. The idea of living in that city seemed like a good fit.

The initial experience of being an assistant coach in the CFL with the Stampeders was a good one. The head coach, Jim Wood, had come from New Mexico State. I didn't know him, but he treated me fairly and gave me a lot of responsibility, coaching both the offensive and defensive lines.

The preseason wasn't much different from what I was used to in college, because we had about 80 players. In the regular season, after we got down to our 32-man roster, things began to change. During our first game, after we had returned a punt, the offensive players started running onto the field. Twelve players were coming off, and 12 were going out—you play 12 guys on each unit in the CFL. I turned around to look at the bench. Only eight guys were left there, and it finally registered how thin our ranks really were.

In the CFL, we had a 24-hour—or 48-hour, I don't recall—time period where we could claim a player on waivers from another team and bring him in, work him out, and make a decision on whether or not we were going to add him to our roster. We did that all the time. First and foremost, we were trying to upgrade our own team. But secondly, we were bringing in guys to work them out, so even if we didn't sign them at that time, we knew something about them. So later, when someone got hurt, we knew which guys we wanted to call in. Because of that experience, to this day I won't hesitate to move a player from offense to defense and play him after only three days' practice.

I don't know if things have changed, but back then a CFL game was played on a field 65 yards wide and 110 yards long. The end zones were 25 yards deep, and they were in play. If the other team kicked a field goal, and you could return it out of the end zone, you could erase the points. If a team punted the ball into the end zone, and the other team couldn't bring it out, that was counted as a single. They used to call it a *rouge*. You could score a point in the kicking game while on defense. The Canadian game was fast. You had only 20 seconds between plays instead of the 25 in American college football. You had no timeouts, except for the last two minutes of the half and the final two minutes of the game. Guys were in motion all over the place.

Players had to line up a yard off the ball, which was a big adjustment for me as a coach. It actually helped me later, because when I returned to college football, the Dallas Cowboys' flex defense was very popular. They'd have a tackle line up a yard or two off the ball and an adjacent lineman right on the ball. The flex defense created some real blocking-angle problems for people. The flex defense filtered down to college ball, but as a coach, I knew how to deal with some of that because of my CFL experience.

In a way, the CFL was my introduction to the spread offense. I was purely a closed-formation guy until I went to Canada and saw all the different formations they used up there. It got me thinking, "Maybe there are other ways to skin a cat."

The CFL had a draft, but it consisted of only Canadian players. At that time, they had what were called "territorial exemptions"—each of the nine teams was allocated two territorial exemptions. Teams would try to locate the best high school talent in their territories and then try to get an American college to sign them to a scholarship, have them play four years of college football, and then get them back as a territorial exemption. That didn't make the college coaches in Canada very happy.

Being a recent college coach who used to be involved in the recruiting process, I took a natural interest in this. When Calgary had a home game on Sunday, I'd go to a high school game on Friday night. I convinced the general manager to have the team put on a clinic and invite some speakers, both Canadian and American coaches. One of our

"I loved the time we spent in Canada. It was a different experience because football is a second sport. There's no real knowledge of football up there. Kids aren't playing little league football, and a lot of the high schools don't play football. The atmosphere at the games was almost more social than sports-oriented. For a while, we lived on about 20 acres. We had cows and horses, and Joe really loved that. I think that was his happiest home time ever."

Arnette Tiller

speakers was Jim Sweeney. We worked out the players, weighed them, measured them, timed them and ran them through some drills. We also invited all the high schools to play at our stadium. Our film guy would shoot the workouts and the games and we sent the film to U.S. colleges to promote the kids. Maybe that was the first combine. A couple of these kids got scholarships, so it ended up being a pretty good deal.

After I had been coaching in Calgary for five years, the assistant general manager in charge of player development decided to go into a different business. The general manager came to me and said, "Tiller, you're good at this stuff, I want you to take this job and get out of coaching." That was during the season, and I wasn't sure I wanted to make that move. After the first of the year, the GM called me at home and said, "This is your last chance." I liked personnel work, and I knew that management was much more stable than coaching, so I took that job.

I've always enjoyed the people side of the business. I think we all have strengths and weaknesses in life, and I certainly have my share of weaknesses. Just ask my wife—she knows. I do think evaluating players is one of my strengths, and I was intrigued with being the director of player personnel. It turned out to be a great experience that allowed me to grow and develop some of my own ideas. I met some great people and coaches visiting various college campuses.

One person I met was Bill Polian, who, at that time, was with the Winnepeg Blue Bombers. He later served on Marv Levy's staff at Montreal, where they won the Grey Cup. He was also with Marv at Buffalo when they went to four Super Bowls, starting out there as the Bills' director of player personnel. Bill became a good friend and has had a great career, most recently with the Indianapolis Colts.

Eventually, managing the stadium became part of my duties, which turned out to be a great experience, and I considered going into facility management.

The country had a Canadian content law, which required a certain percentage of airtime on radio and television be dedicated to Canadian artists. The music of choice in western Canada was country and western. Living in that environment for five or six years, I kind of got out of the rock-n-roll listening mode. So what happened? The first concert I booked for our stadium was Alice Cooper. There were major concerns about protecting the artificial turf, so we laid down fire-resistant tarps on the field. After about three or four meetings with the promoter, I finally was able to assure the stadium society that the turf would be protected. With everything appearing to be a go, I said to the promoter, "Tell me, exactly what kind of music does *she* play?" I didn't know who Alice Cooper was. I was out of touch with the rock stuff, so I thought Alice Cooper was a female.

That was my first experience with a big-name entertainer. We converted the locker room into a dressing room. We had to cover the lockers with red velvet drapes, carpet the concrete floor, and bring in couches and floor lamps. We supplied plenty of caviar and provided cases of Absolut and Cutty Sark.

Finally, it was the night of the concert. The opening act was going on and on, and it started drizzling. I said to the promoter, who was dealing with Alice Cooper's manager, "You've got to get this guy on stage, and you've got to get him up there now."

But Alice Cooper was on the phone, talking to his psychologist in New York. When he was ready to go on, he couldn't find the boa constrictor that was part of his act. It turns out they had left the snake in their limousine and during the night it had turned cool, so the snake had wiggled its way up through the dash and was curled up on the manifold.

That night, I developed an appreciation for a great entertainer. This guy was at the top of his profession, and he was a world-recognized entertainer. There were two security guards on either side of him as he made his way to the stage. Once the music started and he began singing, he put on one heck of a show. He was up there a long, long time, and the audience loved him. When the show ended, those same two security guys grabbed him as he reached the edge of the stage and literally lifted him and ran with him to the limo. They put him in the back seat, and the limo took off. The stadium was located on a highway with a median, but they started out in the wrong direction, so the driver drove over the median, turned around, and headed off to the airport. What an experience that was.

After that, I helped book probably the best concert I've ever been around—The Eagles, during their heyday. We also had country acts, such as Charlie Rich. His opening act was Barbie Benton, Hugh Heffner's former girlfriend, who was trying to get into country music. She had a decent voice, but she really didn't have the range. She never made it big time, but she was good enough to be an opening act. And, of course, she was very easy on the eyes.

We also booked the Billy Graham Crusade, which was a weeklong undertaking. We put hundreds of phones in our press box for people to take pledges. We had multiple meetings to coordinate bus parking. There were so many people wanting to come from so far away that it was buses only. Our entire lot was full of buses each night Graham was there. His group was extremely well organized, extremely professional. Prior to getting involved, I was suspicious of religious groups—specifically, their motives regarding finances. When the Billy Graham group left, I was relieved and very impressed with his organization, because a percentage of the pledges they received went back to those churches that brought people to see him. The majority of the money pledged stayed in the region.

I'll never forget meeting Billy Graham. He was a big football fan and knew some of our players. It was the first time I actually felt moved—as if I were in the presence of a spiritual man. The aura about the man was impressive. I'd never seen anybody before, and I've never seen anybody since who compared to him.

I became intrigued with my job and started going to facility management conventions, but little did I know that I soon would return to coaching, even though I had been an assistant GM less than a year.

In September of 1976, Gary Hopson, the GM who hired me, died unexpectedly of a heart attack, which was traumatic, because our families were very close. Roy Jennings, another friend and vice president of the board, became the interim GM for the remainder of that season. He was on the job only two weeks when the board of directors, which ran the Stampeders organization, decided it needed to replace the coach.

They came to me and said, "We want you to become the head coach." My response was, "Well, I don't think I really want to do that. I think I want to be a GM."

I've appreciated everything I've ever received in life, but for me agreeing to take over the coaching job, my "bonus" was a couple of round-trip airline tickets to Windsor, so we could go back and visit our family. And they adjusted my salary by a couple hundred bucks a month. Everything was understood to be temporary. We had played 10 games, so there were six games left. I don't remember our record, but we might have been 0-10.

On Thursday, three days before our next game, the team president told the coaches and players that I was going to be the head coach for the rest of the season. So I understandably had unhappy assistants and a team that hadn't won; so a lot of the guys were making their plans for the winter. We got thumped that Sunday, and I felt really inadequate because I couldn't even put in one play for that game.

I decided to try to have some fun with the situation since we needed to draw more people to our games. They'd just fired the head coach, but they were required to pay him for the rest of the current season and all of the next season. They owed him around $120,000, which wasn't a huge amount of money. I figured, at 18 dollars a ticket, if we could sell 10,000 more tickets for our last four home games—that's only 2,500 more tickets per game—we had enough money to pay the guy off. The team had a radio show, and to try to get more people in the stands, I would fib and say that I was going to run a play of the week submitted by a fan. I'd make something up about a fan and the play. It was always a deceptive (trick play). Some of them worked, and some of them didn't work, but people started sending in plays, so we had some fun.

That season, Ottawa ended up winning the East, and Edmonton won the West. We played Edmonton—when they were like 14-2 and we were maybe 2-14—and we beat them. We went to Ottawa, and we beat or tied them, I don't remember. So people started coming to our games. Our crowds improved, and they paid off the former head coach. Everything was just lovely.

After I took over, we ended up 2-3-1, and there was a little bit of a media campaign urging the team to name me the permanent head coach. I knew that a GM had a better chance of surviving longer than a coach, so I told them I didn't want to coach. I really liked coaching, but I was trying to leverage into what I thought was a better paying and more secure job.

Calgary was interested in hiring Jack Gotta, who had won one or two Grey Cups—the CFL's championship—at Ottawa. When three guys on our board went to interview Jack, they wanted me there so I could talk about the players, so he would know what kind of team he was going to get.

We were interviewing in a hotel room, and Jack said, "Excuse me, I'd like to talk to just the president and the vice president." We had a suite, so they went into the next room and Jack told them, "I'll take your job, but the only way I'll take it is if I'm both the head coach and the GM." Calgary hadn't named me the GM, but the initial plan was to hire a head coach and then I would become the general manager. They came back into the room and asked me what I thought of Jack's proposal.

Like a fool I said, "If you guys think he's the best man for the job, and that's what it takes to get him, don't worry about me." They said they'd offer him the deal, but only if he kept me as assistant general manager. They covered me, but there was no guarantee. If he didn't like me after a year, he could can me.

We got along pretty well. As the GM, it was Jack's responsibility to sign everybody. I would sign the rookies, because I was the personnel director who dealt with the first-year guys, and he would sign all the veterans. But, as the head coach, he didn't want any ill feelings, so I started taking over the tough cases.

We had two or three seasons where we finished around 14-2 but never made it to the Grey Cup. After that, management decided to bring in a banker to be the CEO of the football operation, and Jack had decided to give up coaching and named one of the assistants to replace him. I didn't like the direction we were headed.

Fortunately, I had stayed in touch with Leon Burtnett, whose first full-time coaching job was at Montana State when I was an assistant coach there. The two of us also were on Coach Sweeney's staff at Washington State.

When Burtnett became the head coach at Purdue in 1982, he called and offered me a job on his staff. I told him, "I can't. I think we're going to restructure here, and I think I'm going to be the GM. That's something I've been working on for five years."

A year later, he again needed a coach as Bobby Cope quit as an assistant at Purdue to become the head coach at Pacific. Leon called me again and said, "Okay, big man, I tried to hire you a year ago, and you wouldn't come. I've got an opening now. Will you come to Purdue?"

So I decided to resign at Calgary. In my letter of resignation, I wrote, "In the armed services, there's a saying that if you don't like the way the unit is being run, don't bitch, just transfer."

I chose to transfer to Purdue.

Chapter 5

A BOILERMAKER FOR THE FIRST TIME

Twenty-five years ago, there weren't assistant head coaches as we have today. However, when I look back at my move to Purdue in 1983—and I've never said this to anyone—everyone probably would have been served better had I been the assistant head coach.

Leon Burtnett wanted to hire me on his staff at Purdue when he first got the job the previous year; but, since I was the assistant general manager of a pro team, there had to be a reason that I'd be interested in the job other than just being an assistant coach. When defensive coordinator Bobby Cope left, Leon said, "If you'll come now, I'll name you the defensive coordinator." I agreed, but if Leon wanted me to come to Purdue with a title, someone else should've been made coordinator and I, the assistant head coach.

I'd been out of coaching for four years, and I had been in Canada for nine years. Things had changed. But Leon wanted me to be his defensive coordinator, and I thought I could do it. I thought we did pretty well at it after a couple years, but I struggled with it early. It was like going back nearly 10 years, when I last coached at the college level.

You take a decade out of your life, out of your career, and things are very different.

I lived with Leon and his family during that first spring, and he did his best to coach me up on the defense. He was the architect of the Junk Defense, and he was recognized as a defensive guru. It was his defense, and he wanted to continue to run that same defense. Since my family was going to stay in Canada until the end of the school year, I moved in with Leon and his family. We'd take film home at night, and he'd coach me. Then we'd watch a game film, and I'd call the defense—but almost two years passed before I was truly comfortable.

We got off to a horrible start at Purdue. My first game as their defensive coordinator was against fifth-ranked Notre Dame, and the Fighting Irish beat us 52-6. It was an inauspicious start, to say the least. After that game was over, I walked back to the locker room thinking, "What have I gotten myself into?"

> "I probably should have put Joe on the offense because he was a hell of an offensive line coach. When he first arrived at Purdue, he lived at my house for about six months, and we would study film and study our defense almost every night—in between eating Haagen-Dazs ice cream. We both gained about 50 pounds because we'd stop at the grocery store each night to get a pint of ice cream, for which, I might add, I always paid.
>
> "I always thought Joe was pretty positive. That didn't mean he didn't get after people, but he never degraded the players. As a coach, you can get after people as long as you don't attack them personally. You're talking to them about the way they're playing football, not about them as a human being. I always thought Joe did a good job in that respect, and that's one reason I liked Joe. When he told the players something they knew it was to make them better, so they would pay attention and respect him for that. Joe was smart enough to know—although we always want to be liked as coaches—it's more important that the players respect you than like you.
>
> "I'm not at all surprised by his success at Purdue. At that time, I don't think defenses knew exactly how to defend his spread offense. Anytime you can do something that nobody else in your league is doing, that's a tremendous advantage. Plus, the fact that Purdue has played such good defense under Brock Spack helped them to a great extent. To run that offense you have to have a good defense because you're not going to take much time off the clock.
>
> "Joe is a good person, and he's done a tremendous job at Purdue."
>
> Leon Burtnett

What I remember most about that game, besides the fact that we took a real lickin', was that we had a young kid named Rod Woodson who, as a true freshman, started at free safety. I'd never seen a true freshman start. When I left college football nine years earlier, freshmen weren't eligible. I couldn't believe that a freshman could play, and Woodson was starting against the No. 5 team in the country. Maybe that's why we gave up 52 points. But certainly Rod went on to become one of the all-time greats at Purdue and, to this day, he's still the best athlete I've ever been around.

Scott Campbell was our quarterback that first year, and the backup was sophomore Jim Everett—a guy we actually discussed moving to another position because he was so big. We thought maybe he'd be a good linebacker or tight end. But the next season, 1984, Everett was our starting quarterback, and we improved from 3-7-1 to 7-5, losing to Virginia 27-24 in the Peach Bowl. That was our only bowl game during my four seasons as a Purdue assistant under Coach Burtnett.

That season, we lost at Miami when the Hurricanes were ranked fifth, but we beat Notre Dame, Michigan, and Ohio State. That's the only time in Purdue history that the Boilermakers have managed to defeat the Fighting Irish, the Wolverines, and the Buckeyes in the same season. Notre Dame was ranked eighth, and Ohio State was ranked second when we played them.

The Notre Dame game that year was one of my most memorable as a coach. Our season opener in Indianapolis was the dedication game for what was then called The Hoosier Dome, and Purdue was a big underdog. Before the game, I was standing in the tunnel leading to the field, toward the back of the team. There was a young linebacker, Fred Strickland, bouncing up and down in front of me. I said to him, "Did you ever dream, a year ago when you were in high school in New Jersey, that you'd be playing against Notre Dame in the Hoosier Dome?" He just shook his head—he was so nervous he couldn't even speak. Strickland may have been as nervous as all get-out before that game, but he ended up being a very good player as a Boilermaker. We won 23-21.

Most of the games at Purdue back then just kind of blend in now. I don't remember much about any of them. Our last season, 1986, certainly was one to forget. We lost six in a row and ended up finishing 3-8. We began to hear rumors about Leon getting fired, which is difficult on an assistant coach, because you know that if they make a change at the top, it involves you as well.

Purdue had been very successful during the five seasons when Leon was the defensive coordinator under Jim Young, going 38-19-1 and winning three consecutive bowl games. Yet, as a head coach, Burtnett was 3-8 and 3-7-1 in his first two seasons before that 1984 bowl season. But then we slipped to 5-6 in 1985 and won just one of seven as we traveled to Evanston to face Northwestern.

George King, the athletic director at the time, and I were on the same bus for that trip, and he began questioning me about what I thought Purdue needed to do to turn the corner in football. He was very professional. He didn't ask me anything about coaching. He didn't back me into a corner, where anything could be interpreted as being disloyal to Leon or anyone else on the staff. In fact, there weren't any questions about coaching.

As a staff, we thought that we were rapidly falling behind in recruiting. That was during the era when Michigan and others, like Ohio State, were building indoor practice facilities. They were among the first, and during recruiting we kept hearing about what we didn't have.

Back then, unlike now, Northwestern was a struggling program, so I thought that it was a measuring-stick game. We couldn't afford to lose that game, or we might be history. But we beat Northwestern, and I thought, "Hey, we're going to come out of the woods and be okay." But then we lost to third-ranked Michigan 31-7 and got spanked 42-14 at Iowa. We came back to beat Indiana, but the decision had been made by then. We actually were told after the Northwestern game that Leon was going to resign, effective at the end of the season.

That Indiana game turned out to be one of the most memorable in Purdue history. It was Woodson's final game as a Boilermaker, and he played both ways—as a defensive back and running back. With

We lived on Old Farm Road in south Lafayette: (left to right) Julie, Arnette, Mike, and Renee. My bike must have been in the trunk! Photo provided by the Joe Tiller family

only two days of practice, I questioned how effective he could be on offense, but he was absolutely outstanding in every phase of the game. As a cornerback, he had 10 tackles, caused a fumble, and broke up a pass. On offense, he rushed 15 times for 93 yards and caught three passes for 87 yards. In addition, he also returned two kickoffs for 46 yards and fielded three punts. Woodson was involved in an incredible 137 plays that day and his iron-man performance helped us edge Indiana 17-15. There was no question in my mind about his athletic prowess, but that performance demonstrated to the world what a great athlete he was.

Coaching those final games was extremely difficult knowing that it was the end of the line. Trying to deal with recruits and trying to coach was very hard. Your personal pride said to keep competing, but your emotions said, "The heck with this, I'm not going to be around, so why put in the hours?" But we kept working hard and went down swinging. At the postseason banquet, they let each coach speak for about two minutes, and I told the players that they should draw on the actions of that coaching staff. Because, to a man, everyone fought the good fight, even as the door was closing on him.

Leon had a lot of pride in his recruiting abilities. He absolutely loved recruiting and was very involved in recruiting some big-name players, such as Woodson and Ray Wallace. In what was to be our last season at Purdue, we were chasing quarterback Jeff George, one of Indiana's all-time great high school players. Leon basically took over the recruiting of Jeff. He won that battle, as George came on board, but that was the year we were doomed.

Purdue's decision to make a change was more difficult than usual for the Tillers because we absolutely loved Lafayette. We lived on Old Farm Road, which was a perfect spot to raise a family. We were totally immersed in the Lafayette community. Arnette had started college at Purdue, and life was good. The only downside was that we weren't winning, and we weren't paid very much. However, if we would have been asked by the next head coach to stay, we would have done so in a minute, because we loved Lafayette.

After we got fired, I eventually took a job as an assistant at Wyoming. I came back to pick up the family after the school year. We were all in the car, and I pulled off Old Farm Road to begin our trip to Wyoming. Our son, Mike, was in the back seat, and he said, with a real sad voice, "Dad, do you think we'll ever live anywhere as nice as Old Farm Road again?"

I thought about that for a few seconds. And then I said, "Mike, probably not." I was just being honest, trying not to hurt his feelings. Our kids were learning how tough life could be for a coach's family.

Chapter 6

A DREAM FINALLY COMES TRUE

Arnette and I went to the coaches' convention in January of 1987 without a job, and we left the convention without a job, although we were in the mix for a couple. I'm a believer in old clichés, that it's not what you know but who you know, that timing in life is everything.

When I first started coaching at Montana State, a guy was on the staff named Dick Roach, and we became good friends. Dick's older brother, Paul, was an assistant at Wyoming. Twenty years later, Paul had become the head coach and athletic director at Wyoming. His first year there was when we were let go at Purdue, so the timing was perfect, and he wanted me to be on his staff. Paul called while we were still at the coaches' convention in San Diego. He wanted to know, on our way back to West Lafayette, if we'd make a side trip to Laramie.

I was getting feelers from people in the CFL due to my experience up there. I also had interviewed for a couple of jobs at the convention, including one as a coordinator at New Mexico, which was in the same league as Wyoming. But we went to visit Paul in Laramie, and he hired me as the offensive line coach. I took the Wyoming job because of Paul

Roach—not because the pay was so great, or because it was a glamorous program. I took the job because of the man, because of the person. It didn't bother me that I wasn't the coordinator, because of my respect for Paul, and I knew he wanted to be involved in the offense. A year later, he did promote me to offensive coordinator, but he still called the plays.

From a football standpoint, those were certainly the best of times. We won back-to-back Western Athletic Conference championships. We were 8-0 in conference play both seasons, and became the first school in WAC history to go undefeated two years in a row in conference play.

At that time, the champion of the WAC automatically earned an invite to play in the Holiday Bowl in San Diego. The second year, the number of tickets sold from the state was about 19,000—which would have made our crowd at the bowl game the fifth-largest city in Wyoming. We played Iowa in our first trip to the Holiday Bowl, losing 20-19 after we had a punt blocked late in the game. Paul Roach has never forgiven the player who was responsible for that block. He can tell you exactly the time of the game, where the penetration came from, and who was responsible for the block.

"During a very tense game against Air Force, I looked to our field goal kicker, Sean Fleming, for the winning kick with little time remaining. He was a freshman back then, and it was rather obvious to me that he was very nervous.

"I was trying to think of some way to calm him down, so I told him, 'Son, this thing was won or lost a long time ago. You don't have anything on your shoulders. Just keep your head down and hit it. If it goes, it goes.'

"Sean looked at me, very excited, and said, 'Thank you, Coach. Thank you.'

"When the team ran back out on the field, I turned to Joe and said, 'What's he thanking me for?'

'Because you told him he didn't have to make it,' Joe told me. But he kicked that field goal, and we won the game 48-45."

Paul Roach

We were a better team the next season, but we had the misfortune of playing a very, very good Oklahoma State team in the Holiday Bowl—the Oklahoma State Cowboys versus the Wyoming Cowboys. One of their Cowboys was a "scrawny" running back by the name of Barry Sanders. We had lost to them during the regular season

Talking to the offensive linemen at Wyoming. Our son, Mike (the cord carrier), is at the left.
Photo porvided courtesy of University of Wyoming

the previous year, so we knew how good they were. During the Holiday Bowl, we knocked Thurman Thomas, their starting running back, out of the game; so we were thinking that we were okay. But they put in Sanders, and he absolutely ran wild. Oklahoma State thumped us 62-14 as Sanders rushed 29 times for 222 yards and a Holiday Bowl-record five touchdowns.

Overall, we were 21-5 so those were a great two years. However, at the end of that second season, Athletic Director Roach negotiated a new contract with Head Coach Roach—and the head coach signed a new 10-year contract. This was in 1988, and I was 46 years old. I figured if I didn't become a head coach before I turned 50 that I probably wouldn't ever be a head coach. Even before that happened, I had already begun to wonder if I was going to be a "lifer"—forever an assistant coach.

When we got canned at Purdue after the 1986 season, a job opened up that I dearly coveted—to become the head coach at Montana State, my alma mater. I never worked as hard in my life trying to get a job. They turned me down, but they did me a great favor by not hiring me. If they would have hired me, I probably never would have left.

When I was in Calgary, after I had gotten out of coaching, I got a call and went for an interview with Monte Clark, the head coach of the Detroit Lions. He wanted me to join his staff as the offensive line coach. I thought that if I could get a job as an assistant coach in the NFL, that's probably where I'd finish my career. I figured I would never become a head coach.

During the interview process, I was watching tape with Clark, and he said, "Now, correct this player on this particular play." I was so excited that I forgot one of the most important things. Whenever I coached, I always would start by looking at a guy's feet. As a line coach, I always was interested in angle of departure. Guess what? I went up there to Detroit, and I was so damned excited that I never even mentioned the guy's feet during my critique. Sure enough, we finished with the interview, and Monte said, "You know, Joe, you did pretty well on this interview; but you never talked about the guy's feet."

I couldn't believe I did that. The Lions were my favorite team as a kid, and I was so enamored with the fact that I was interviewing with the franchise. I was like a kid about ready to pee my pants just thinking about being in the Lions' office, and I had a chance to be one of their coaches. Are you kidding me? No kid who grows up on Collomore Road has a chance to coach the Detroit Lions. It just doesn't happen.

Clark interviewed a couple more guys and didn't offer me the job. That was a lucky break, because I would have taken it. Monte was a former line coach for Don Shula at Miami during their Super Bowl years. There's a rule in coaching: "Never coach the position that the head coach coaches, because no matter how you do it, you're not going to do it as well." Also, I didn't know Monte, and that would have been a violation of my underlying philosophy of going with the right person, not the prestige of the job. As it turned out, the Lions fired Clark a year or two later. More than one NFL coach told me that, although Monte was a very good coach, he wasn't the easiest man in the world to work for.

Our stay in Canada was a very good deal for us, but we stayed too long. It was like, 'out of sight, out of mind.' If you go to Canada to coach, you have to really work at staying in touch with your contacts, because they'll forget you. You can go to Canada, pick up some experience for three or four years, but then you should move on. While you're there, you need to be working on your next job, which I've never done well. Thank God, Leon Burtnett hired me at Purdue—not many people would do that.

The good thing about Canada was that we met some great people, lifelong friends. We loved the West. We loved putting on our cowboy boots and going to the Calgary Stampede (a rodeo) every year. Our son was born there. Although the length of our stay was a setback on my career, in the process I picked up invaluable experience as a coach and in management. I look for the same qualities in a player when I evaluate them today thanks to my time evaluating personnel.

As I started getting older, I began to look at things from a head coach's point of view. Whomever I worked for at the time, I thought loyalty was paramount; so, I never questioned the head coach and always supported him, both publicly and privately. But in the back of my mind, I would always judge each of his decisions and ponder whether I'd have done things differently.

Closing in on 50, I found myself again thinking, "If I don't become a head coach pretty soon, I'm going to be a lifer." Watching and seeing who was getting head coaching positions, I became depressed when I realized that their pedigrees were better than mine. Guys of style, not necessarily guys of substance, were getting jobs. But that made me think I could do it. I told Arnette that I thought I'd be a better head coach than I was an assistant coach. I never considered getting out of coaching because I was confident that something would happen. I never questioned my coaching ability—just whether I'd ever get the chance.

During my first stint at Washington State, Coach Sweeney had hired a young coach by the name of Mike Price. Arnette was so excited because Mike and his wife, Joyce, were the first people who were younger than we were on any staff we had been on.

Fast-forward to 1989, and Mike's the head coach at Washington State, putting his staff together. He called me and offered me everything he could to get me to go to Washington State. He offered me $16,000 more than I was making at Wyoming. Back then, when you were making $40,000, and somebody offered you $56,000, that was a lot of money. I was earning about as much at Wyoming as I had been making at Purdue—the only difference was that it was four years later. Wyoming paying the same amount as Purdue was somewhat amazing, since Wyoming had a 33,000-seat stadium, and Purdue had a 65,000-seat stadium.

Mike wanted me to be the offensive coordinator and coach the offensive line. He also offered to make me the assistant head coach, but I said I'd rather have the money, so that's what he gave me. When I told Paul Roach about the offer, he thought I was going to Washington State for the interview. I didn't need the interview. I didn't need to check out Pullman. I'd already coached there. I knew Mike, and I knew the guys on his staff—and he'd told me everything I needed to know.

So Paul immediately said, "How much are you making here?"

I told him, and he said, "You know, I was going to give you a pretty good bump this year."

So I finally spelled it out and told him, "No, Paul, I'm going there to work."

His first response was, "You can't do that. You can't leave us like this." He asked if I'd stick around a few days and coach the new coach, so I agreed; but then I returned to coach at Washington State for the second time.

The next season I interviewed for the head coaching job at Toledo. I was one of the finalists, but they eventually hired Nick Saban. Back at Washington State, we had recruited a pretty good quarterback named Drew Bledsoe to come in for our second year there. Things were starting to happen for me. I thought, "We've got Drew Bledsoe; and if we can put up some good numbers and do some good things, I'm going to get a shot at a head coaching job."

> "Joe's got his own style. He's kind of a thinking man's football coach. He's very analytical and very smart. He's a real good teacher. He had a tough way about him, but I think we all mellow with age. Maybe he used to scream it, and now he says it. But he's always going to do something to make you better."
>
> Mike Price

And then it happened. At the end of that year, Paul Roach decided to retire as head coach at Wyoming and devote all his energies to being the athletic director. He called me at Washington State, and I'll never forget that conversation.

He began by asking, "Joe, would you ever think about coming back to Wyoming?"

My response was, "As what?" He hadn't yet announced that he was getting out of coaching.

He said, "Well, as the head coach."

I instantly blurted out, "I can't be there for at least another 20 minutes or so."

I went to Laramie the next week, and he offered me the job. That was the easiest interview I've ever had in my life. I quickly accepted his offer. When I left Paul's house to drive back to the airport, I couldn't believe what had just happened. I was going to be a head coach—what I had worked for all my life. I was about to live my dream.

My daydreaming was abruptly interrupted when a cop pulled up behind me and turned on his flashers. I was driving 45 in a 25-mph zone. He drove up to get even with me, but then he waved his hand and motioned for me to slow down. I did, but it was hard to do, as I was so excited.

Head Coach Joe Tiller!

Chapter 7

COWBOY JOE

During the press conference to introduce me as the Wyoming head coach, Paul Roach did something that I really appreciated. He told everyone work needed to be done, that the talent level was not what it had been. He said there were personnel issues with both the coaches and players—that Wyoming fans needed to be patient.

Quite a statement by an athletic director who was previously the head coach—not many guys would say that. But he hit the nail right on the head. In 1990, Paul's final season as coach of the Cowboys, they had finished 9-4, winning their first nine games but losing the final four, including a 17-15 loss to California in the Copper Bowl. But when I took over, there wasn't a particularly large senior class, and the recruiting had fallen off in some of the lower classes. Paul Roach hired me because he knew me, and he believed that we could work together. He was comfortable with me coming in and making the necessary changes.

We kind of struggled for a couple of years; and then, I'll be darned if we didn't end up tied for the WAC championship in our third season. We had to win at San Diego State in the final game of the season to claim a share of the title. We were the underdogs but ended up winning, 43-38. Even though we tied BYU for the title, they won the tiebreaker and went to the Holiday Bowl.

Laramie was small enough that I had a listed telephone number, and, when we got back from that trip, I had a message on my phone from LaVell Edwards, the head coach at Brigham Young.

I was surprised that LaVell would call me. It was just our third year in the league, and I really didn't know him that well. He was the wily ol' veteran who had dominated that league. Coach Edwards called to congratulate us on winning the game and said he was glad to share the championship with us. And then he said, "By the way, I never said that I'd rather lose and live in Utah than win and live in Wyoming." I later asked some media guys, and they claimed that he did say it. We had the misfortune of drawing an upstart Kansas State team, coached by Bill Snyder, in the Copper Bowl and lost, 52-17. We then slipped to 6-6 and 6-5 the next two seasons.

Things went pretty much the way I thought they would my first few years as a head coach. I always believed that I would do well, so I ran the program the way I thought it should be run. I made some mistakes, but I learned a lot during my stay at Wyoming, especially that first season. I was really a hardnosed coach back then, and I was too hard on those players. Everything was right to the letter—no leeway of any sort.

"There are two sides to Joe Tiller. He's a big guy who looks tough, and at times, he can be tough. On the other side, he has a pleasing and congenial personality. He also possesses a dry sense of humor, which, at times, makes him really funny.

"Because of his personality, he gets along very well with people. He relates well. He's accepted well, and he has great character. What you see is what you get with Joe."

Paul Roach

"Joe really has a laid-back sense of humor. When he was appointed the head coach at Wyoming, at our first league coaches meeting, I got up and said, 'I'm now the oldest coach in the league, but I'm no longer the most bald-headed guy in the league.'

"And Joe got up, rubbed the top of his head, and said, 'My wife refers to this as the solar-powered sex machine.'"

LaVell Edwards

I began to change, though, becoming less emotional. That year was the first time I really saw myself, and I thought, "Hey, Tiller, you better back off and ease up a little bit. You're such a hard-nosed guy, you're like a drill sergeant. You need to be a little more compassionate."

The real transformation took place our third year at Wyoming, the first year we won the championship. That was the year I really became calmer and realized that running up and down the sideline screaming all the time was not the way to coach. So I made a conscious effort to find the right coaching style for me. It was a three-year process. I didn't change overnight, but I began to evaluate everything I did—in the meeting rooms, on the practice field, and during the games. I became much more of a players' coach—however, some would say not enough.

In our third year, we weren't having any fun. I walked into the room for our Thursday night meeting, and all I saw was a bunch of long faces—guys looking like they weren't enjoying football. It hit me right between the eyes. By now, we had recruited most of those players, so I decided that our primary goal for the rest of that week was to have fun. I told the coaches that I didn't want to hear one negative word on a headset or on the sideline during that Saturday's game. I'll be damned if we didn't win the game and went on to tie for the championship.

Those first three years at Wyoming were when I made the biggest changes, from being very involved—I don't want to say from being ballistic—to being very calm on the sideline. And I've been that way ever since. Sometimes it's difficult, but as I get older, it seems to be easier.

"During his first seasons as a head coach at Wyoming, when I was around 14, I would carry his cord, so I was on his hip the entire game. The first couple of years, he would brutally rip the officials. Stuff came out of his mouth that would make a hooker blush.

"During one game against Hawaii, he just absolutely ripped an official—personal attacks and everything. I probably spent most of the fourth quarter alongside my dad, just following this official up and down the field, ripping into him. Sure enough, that crew kept calling stuff against Wyoming. The next season, my dad shut up. Now when there's a bad call, he says maybe two or three strong words to the official and then walks away."

Mike Tiller

Still, there are times when I want to pull my hair out, and I want to jump a player. There are times when I want to get in their face and really chew on them; but, for the most part, I don't. I just don't. I think positive is more effective than negative, especially with today's young people.

Coaching at Wyoming was a lot of fun. Recruiting there was so unique. Our recruiting base actually was the state of Colorado. When we left Wyoming to come to Purdue, almost 30 of the 80 players on our roster were from Colorado. We'd always go up into Montana, because the state of Montana didn't have a Division I program—neither did Idaho nor the Dakotas. The recruits from low-population states like Wyoming, Montana, and North and South Dakota thought Laramie looked like their hometowns. We couldn't build a team from just those states, but every year we'd get a handful of recruits from them. Our recruits from the state of Wyoming were mostly walk-ons. At that time, Wyoming only had 56 high schools that played football, and some of those didn't even play 11-man football. They only had one league that was a Triple A (large school) conference. We filled out our roster with northern California junior-college players, never having much luck in southern California—and I didn't enjoy recruiting there.

Recruiting was a challenge. We had to do extensive research to find that diamond in the rough. We won our first championship with Joe Hughes at quarterback, a junior-college transfer out of Butte College in northern California. His family lived in rural northern California. When we went for the home visit, there was a bass boat sitting in the front yard, and a black lab was on the front porch wagging his tail at us. In the house, some mounted ducks were hanging on the wall. I looked at the assistant coach who was with me and said, "I think we have a chance here."

Some of the most unusual stories about recruiting at Wyoming involve the players we lost. If another school was in the mix, we usually didn't get the guy—unless it was a Division II or

Division III school. We even lost recruits to Division I-AA schools.

There was this one kid from Arizona, a big, good-looking tackle. His family was Mormon, and he wanted to go to Brigham Young. But we had him in for a campus visit, and I went to do a home visit. He had taken an official trip to Brigham Young, and they didn't offer him a scholarship. It got down to the final week of recruiting, and he was still waiting for Brigham Young's offer. Finally, the night before signing day, we called him, and he said, "Coach, I've decided that I'm not going to go to college."

We lost that kid to nobody.

One of the craziest recruiting trips was a one-day marathon, flying from Wyoming to Denver, then to Kansas City for a home visit. Then it was on to Toronto for another home visit. After that, I flew to Tulsa, where an assistant coach picked me up and drove me to rural Oklahoma for a home visit that night. We thought we were going to get this kid; but at the house, the mother just sat there and filed her nails. She never said a word. Both the father and the boy were very nice—everything was, "Yes, sir; no, sir." It was a week before signing day, and we knew he didn't have any offers, so I was asking this kid to commit.

Finally, his dad said his son was going to stay close to home. He's going up to such and such a town. I thought, "What the hell's there?" Well, it was Northeastern Oklahoma Junior College. He chose to go to a junior college instead of playing at Wyoming.

We'd lost a guy to nobody and then a guy to a junior college.

On another home visit—I don't recall where—I was talking to the kid about committing, and he said, "Coach, I've made my decision. I'm going to Army." I was stunned, so I asked him, "You've got an appointment to West Point?" The kid said, "No, I'm going to join the army."

So we'd lost a kid to nobody, lost a kid to a junior college, and lost another one to the army.

The tables were reversed on another trip. In northern California, where we had recruited some good players, we were trying to recruit a youngster by the name of Waymon Levingston. It was a military family, and their home was on a military base. Waymon was a very sharp young man and had received appointments to West Point and Annapolis. He had visited the U.S. Naval Academy and received an offer. But during our home visit, Waymon told us he would sign with Wyoming. When he committed to us, his mother looked stunned. The next thing I knew, there were tears rolling down her face. I felt so bad. But Waymon, who was a little guy, came to Wyoming and started three years for us.

One year, there were four good players in Wyoming, but they all ended up going out of state, to schools like Stanford, UCLA, and Colorado. I found it unique that, when we went into those communities, people were glad to see the University of Wyoming recruiting there. When we talked to the people at the high schools, however, most of them were more excited for their player having the opportunities to go somewhere outside of Wyoming. I thought that was strange since we were the state institution, we were recruiting a guy, and yet everyone wanted him to leave. I never understood that, and I always have had a problem with that line of thinking.

During our third or fourth year at Wyoming, the football staff decided to go around the state and put on mini-clinics for younger kids. When we showed up in these small towns, we had to look a little bit like the Clampett family from *The Beverly Hillbillies* television series—our university pickup with tackling dummies in the back followed by a van containing the coaches. They were all-day clinics, trying to teach a little football but making it a fun thing to do. We conducted these camps for about three years, each year going to different parts of the state.

The fund-raising arm for the athletic department at Wyoming is called the "Cowboy Joe Club." One spring, we went on a mini-tour to visit several towns for lunch or dinner, usually traveling hundreds of miles, trying to raise money for the athletic department. A gathering in the town of Worland was held in the back of a bar. We set up right next to some guys who were playing poker. I was trying to give an update on the team, but I had to talk over the poker players, who were screaming and yelling and wouldn't stop their card game while we gave our presentation—only in Wyoming. In the little town of Lusk, the crowd was so small—I think there were about a dozen people there—I didn't even stand up. We all just sat around a table and visited over a cup of coffee. There was no formal program at all. I loved it.

On another one of these trips—I believe it was in Torrington—we were going to have a fundraising auction, which had been very successful in the past. We pulled into town and went to visit a guy who ran a grain elevator because he wanted to donate to the auction. The guy looked around his store and said, "Grab a couple bags of that lawn fertilizer." So I grabbed a 40-pound bag of lawn fertilizer, along with one of my assistants, who turned to me and said, "Joe, you suppose Tom Osborne is out there in Nebraska right now picking up a bag of fertilizer?" That put everything in perspective—the joys of coaching in Wyoming. At the time, I wouldn't have traded it for anything.

Even traveling to games as a team was exciting at Wyoming. My first season, we had a game scheduled at Colorado—the year after they shared the national championship with Georgia Tech. We couldn't find a place to stay—the closest was about halfway between Laramie and Boulder. So Paul Roach asked me, "What do you think about just driving down there, playing the game, and driving back?" That drive usually took nearly three hours, but I signed off on the plan. Only one hotel-restaurant would take us for our pregame meal, but it wasn't large enough to accommodate the team in their dining area; so about a third of us actually had our pregame meal in their bar, sitting in semi-circle booths.

Those players were the most unpretentious guys I've ever been around—I just loved them. You could give them their pregame meal

"When we were at Wyoming, we were in the weight room and I said, 'Coach, we've got some guys here with their shirts untucked.' He looked at me and said, 'We're on these guys' asses all the time. We're on them to go to class; we're all over them on the football field; so we've got to give them latitude to be a kid.' I played for him, so I knew how he was, and that kind of took me by surprise. Then I thought, 'What does that really have to do with winning or losing a football game?' I realized that he was very disciplined, but he gives players some room to be themselves. He does that with coaches as well. I've been amazed at his patience."

Brock Spack

in a brown paper bag, and they wouldn't complain. They just wanted to play football. We bused to the stadium, and although Colorado beat us 30-13, our guys actually played a heck of game. The score was 20-13 in the fourth quarter.

During my fourth season at Wyoming, we played at Nebraska—ironically, the year after the Cornhuskers shared the national championship with Michigan. We scored first, and I had a flashback to when I was an assistant at Purdue and Lee Corso was the head coach at Indiana. One time, his team scored first against Ohio State, and he called a timeout to have his picture taken with the scoreboard in the background showing: "Indiana 7, Ohio State 0."

So after we scored first, I was yelling for us to call a timeout, but the assistant coaches talked me out of it. I'll be damned if we didn't score again to make it 14-0. Again, I started screaming to call a timeout but we never did. We were leading at halftime, but I never did get that picture. All we did was make them mad—they scored three times in the third quarter. Yet, we scored again, and it was a three-point game with three minutes to go—but we dropped a punt, they recovered on the 12-yard line, and beat us by 10 points, 42-32.

After that game, I witnessed one of the strangest things I've ever seen as a football coach. A crowd of Nebraska fans, lined up three, four, and five deep along the route we had to take to get to our locker room applauded us as we walked by them.

Before the 1996 season, my final year at Wyoming, the WAC decided to expand from 10 to 16 teams and split into two eight-team divisions. Part of the reason for that was to create a larger television market. That lasted only two years, though; and then eight schools left

In 1993, besides being the head coach, I became actively involved in coaching the offensive line.
Photo provided courtesy of University of Wyoming

the WAC and formed a new league. We had a good team that year, going 10-1 to win the Pacific Division. We played LaVell Edwards' BYU team in the playoff game in front of a sellout crowd in Las Vegas.

It was a heck of a game. We had a five-point lead near the end and chose to take a safety. We had the leading punter in the league, but I just thought, "We've got a five-point lead, and if we punt from our own end zone, and they score, they win the game. So let's do something strategic. Let's do something really smart. Let's take a safety, which puts them within three. A field goal will tie, but we've got the league's top punter and a pretty good defense, so let's punt from our 20-yard line and play defense."

The referee blew the ball ready for play, but our punter, Aron Langley, stood there with the ball, kind of looking around. It was a full house, it was loud, and he never heard the whistle. I yelled from the sidelines, "Punt it, Aron! Punt it!" The play clock was ticking down— seven, six, five. I'm pointing at the clock, so he looked over his shoulder, and there was only two seconds left. We were about to take a five-yard penalty for delay of game, so he turned back at the field and just got the punt off in time—but it went only about 30 yards. I thought for sure we would pin them down inside their 40, maybe inside their 30. Instead, the ball was at midfield. With only a few seconds left, they kicked a field goal and tied it. I learned a good lesson after that—never take a negative-yardage play in overtime, particularly on your first play. If you're throwing the ball, do not take a sack. I can't remember too much about the rest of that game, but we ended up losing in overtime.

That game was played December 10, 1996, and we actually took the Purdue job the last week of November, which had been announced. However, people overwhelmingly believed I owed it to Wyoming to coach this team, to coach that game, and I agreed. The two athletic directors got together and worked out a deal that allowed me to coach the Cowboys in that playoff game.

The players we had at Wyoming were great to be around because they didn't take themselves too seriously. They didn't come to

After beating San Diego State at their place, and winning our first of two championships at Wyoming, two Montana guys carried me off the field, Cody Kelly (left) and Greg Scanlon. Photo provided courtesy of University of Wyoming

Wyoming with the thought of becoming NFL players. They came to play Division I football—and they were excited about it. That was very refreshing and made my stay at Wyoming very enjoyable.

Wyoming has a reputation of being a stepping-stone job. They had multiple coaches—Bob Davaney, Pat Dye, Fred Akers, and Dennis Erickson—who used the position as a springboard. Wyoming is unique because, after you're gone, the people seem to like you more than they did when you were there. If you go on to have some success, they really want to claim you as one of theirs, which is also neat. There seems to be a kind of kinship—that feeling that, once you're there, you're always one of their guys.

I certainly haven't worked at football citadels, but we enjoyed every community we've ever been in. We've formed some lifelong friendships at every stop. My career has been somewhat unusual: I played at Montana State, and then I coached at Montana State. I was twice an assistant at Washington State. I coached at Wyoming as an assistant and then went back there as a head coach. I coached at Purdue as an assistant and then came back as a head coach. I was drafted by Calgary as a player, and, 15 years later, I went back as a coach. I either wear well, or the people I've worked for aren't the sharpest tacks in the box. I say that tongue-in-cheek as I suspect and hope the former is true.

We truly loved the state of Wyoming, the people and the geography—so much so that, when we started discussing where we were ultimately going to land, we settled on the acreage we bought outside of Buffalo, a little town in northern Wyoming. I always thought we'd go back to Bozeman, Montana, where I went to college and then coached for seven years. I spent 11 consecutive years in Bozeman. That's where I met Arnette, and her family is from Belgrade, just a few miles up the road.

At around the age of 50, we started talking about how we needed to think about calling some place home. We liked the Rocky Mountains, so we figured we would end up in Montana or Wyoming.

We also considered Idaho; and we liked Colorado, but we thought it was growing too fast. After looking for four years, we finally bought a place two miles outside of Buffalo—so we're headed back to Wyoming someday. We love the people, and we love the country.

Chapter 8

MOVIN' ON UP TO THE BIG TEN

Purdue's first call came from Jim Colletto, who had announced, with three games remaining, that he was leaving as the Boilermakers' head coach at the end of that 1996 season. Jim helped Purdue Athletic Director Morgan Burke formulate a list of candidates, and he called and asked me if I'd be interested in the job. My response was, "Should I be?" Colletto answered with, "Well, it pays well."

It paid well if you weren't being paid very much—and I wasn't being paid very much. I actually took a pay cut in my base salary as an assistant to become the head coach at Wyoming. I was making $68,000 at Washington State as the assistant head coach, and I went to Wyoming for a base salary of $65,000, although I also received a housing allowance of $1,000 a month and another $10,000 to do radio and television shows, speak at the weekly quarterback club, and attend athletic department golf outings. When I left Wyoming, I was making about $112,000.

Coach Colletto told me there was no question that Purdue was behind many schools in the Big Ten. Jim and I had been on the same staff at Purdue under Leon Burtnett in the mid-1980s, so that didn't come as a surprise to me. But Jim recommended that I at least speak with Morgan, and Purdue was intriguing to me because I had been there before.

About a week after Coach Colletto announced his resignation, Morgan called. We still had a couple of games to play at Wyoming, which was interesting, because I had never been involved in anything like that before; and other jobs started opening. The Minnesota and Illinois jobs broke, and I got calls from both of them—not from the athletic directors but from one of the headhunters who often do a lot of the preliminary work. At that time, we were undefeated; and I really wanted to coach out the season because we were having a hell of a year, and I thought we would be able to finish strong.

I didn't really know, or care, who else Purdue was interviewing. I didn't pay much attention to it because things were moving quickly, and it seemed as if I was getting a call from another school every day. I'll give Morgan credit: he was the most aggressive of anyone who called me. He had a job open, and he wanted to fill it quickly. That those other jobs were open and my name was being circulated—with the media beginning to call—might have prompted him to move quickly.

At Wyoming that season, although we qualified for the first-ever WAC championship game, we finished our regular season a week before most programs. Morgan and Purdue Associate Athletic Director Roger Blalock flew out to meet me in Cheyenne, Wyoming. I just dismissed myself for a couple hours that day and didn't tell anybody where I was going. We met for a couple hours, but I didn't think that much of it, to be honest. They talked about what they were prepared to offer a coach, but they didn't say they were offering me. It was substantially more than I was making at Wyoming, but it wasn't, by today's standards, a knockout contract.

What impressed me the most, financially, was the bonus system they had. Things have changed today; but at that time, they were having a very difficult time putting fannies in the seats, so they had created an attendance bonus. I looked at that and began to figure matters as if we could fill the stadium. I thought, "Wow, I could get a $200,000 check at the end of the season if we could fill that thing." That was unbelievable. I couldn't imagine a kid from a dead-end street in Toledo, Ohio, getting that kind of money. I had never even seen a check for that amount.

They weren't prepared at that time to offer me the job, and I wasn't prepared to accept if they had offered it. So they said they would give me a call, and they headed back. I'm sure they were looking at other guys, such as Glen Mason, who was at Kansas at the time; and Bob Davie, who was the assistant head coach at Notre Dame. In all probability, I was not their first choice, but that didn't bother me. I was very relaxed and very comfortable, and the meeting went well. I knew more about Purdue than I did some of these other jobs. At that time of year, the college job market is just beginning to heat up, so I wasn't chomping at the bit to get the Purdue job, because I knew other openings would surface.

I don't really recall the progression of how things played out, but some of the other schools began inquiring about whether I would visit and interview. I really didn't want to do that. Although we really liked and enjoyed Wyoming, I had already made the decision, before we had any job offers, that we were leaving Wyoming. They had a new athletic director, Lee Moon, who hadn't hired me, and we really didn't have much to do with each other. He came on board in August, and we started the season a week later. As the season went along, I found out more and more about him from other people. I got along with Lee, but there wasn't much about the football program for him to critique. We were having a great season, so he couldn't say, "You ought to change this, or you might want to change that." But that's the kind of guy he was, a very hands-on athletic director. He had been a coach himself; he had a lot of opinions about coaching; and I wasn't his guy. Although I got along well with him, I just knew that it wasn't going to work. I wasn't his hire, and his management style was not something I would've been comfortable with, so the time was right. We needed to move on.

Morgan had called Lee to get permission to interview me, and Lee told me—I don't know how he knew, maybe he was just guessing—that he thought I was their guy. He said, "I think they're going to offer you the job." That's when rumors about bowl bids were starting up, and Lee wanted to know, "If you took another job, would you be able to coach Wyoming in a bowl game?" I told him, "I love those kids, and I'd like to stay because of them." He asked me about the playoff game, and I told him I'd definitely stay for that.

When Morgan decided he wanted to hire me, he didn't drag his feet. He put a contract together and wanted me to take a trip to Purdue with Arnette to meet with the university president and the president of the board of trustees. He wanted it all done now. Everything was moving a little fast for me, but I finally decided, "The heck with all this job market stuff, maybe Purdue is the right place for us." We'd been there, we knew the community, and we had friends there. It was an easy move—it was the Big Ten.

I called Morgan and I told him not to overreact to any rumors he might hear about me and other jobs. I think my exact words to him were, "If you offer us this job, we're not going to leave you standing at the altar."

After our last regular-season game, Morgan called and asked if we'd be his guests for Purdue's last game, against Indiana. I agreed, and when I came to Purdue, it was basically a formality. The contract was all made up, and I signed it on Sunday—the day after the Indiana game—before I was formally announced as the new coach. At the press conference, I made the statement that we planned to win right away, that "... we weren't going to take forever to figure this out. We've won in the past, and we'll win in the future."

I said that not to brag but to exude confidence. I felt that the Purdue team probably needed someone to say that. I had learned as a head coach that every team is about as good as its senior class, so I was telling our seniors that we owe them our best coaching effort. We shouldn't be focused on the future; we should be focused on the present. We thought that we had a decent system, and if we could get in there and get it implemented that maybe we would have some measurable degree of success.

I didn't expect to have as much success so quickly at Purdue, but the schedule was friendly since we didn't play Michigan or Ohio State our first two seasons. At that time, we were the only team using the one-back, spread offense in the Big Ten. Others were dabbling in it, but we were using it exclusively. The entire premise of the spread offense is to balance out the field. When you close up your formation, it becomes a game of strength. The more condensed your formation is, the more significant the physical part of the game becomes. When you spread the formation out, and make the opponent play you in space, it becomes more of a finesse game. We believed coming into the Big Ten and playing a finesse game would benefit us. Quite frankly, we didn't know to what degree it would benefit us. Would it allow us just to be competitive, or would it allow us to win some games?

Coach Colletto was under some pressure to produce a winning season heading into his final year with the Boilermakers. After all, it was his sixth season at Purdue, and, counting Jim's last year, the program had struggled through 12 consecutive losing seasons. I think he probably was forced into a compromising position, dealing with some team discipline issues. Some issues aren't visible throughout the course of the season, but, if they're ignored, they always nip you in the butt on Saturday afternoon.

I really liked Jim when we were on Leon Burtnett's staff at Purdue in the mid-1980s. I think Jim is a good coach, but I think after you're in a job five years and don't have a winning season, you're at the end of the rope. Perhaps you tend to look the other way one season. That's a human tendency. But when you come in new, the bar has yet to be set. You're the one who's going to set the bar, so you're able to do some things that the previous group couldn't accomplish. After having talked with many folks surrounding the Purdue program, one of the most identifiable problems was a needed attitude adjustment.

When you are the new sheriff in town, it's much easier to come in and clean up a situation than when you're the same guy wearing the same hat. I'm not sure we were saying anything that was drastically different from the previous coaching staff, but since we were new faces with new voices, the players probably listened a little more intently. Our first year at Purdue, we started the fall camp with 19 fewer scholarship players on the team than when we arrived. They were the guys who weren't buying into the philosophy of the program. Maybe cleansing is too strong of a word, maybe it isn't, but we had some guys who had bad attitudes, which was part of the reason they weren't reaching their potential as a team.

We were getting a late start in recruiting because, remember, we signed with Purdue and then actually went back to Wyoming and coached in that playoff game on December 10. The first week on the job, I scheduled 15-minute interviews with every player on the team. Most people probably thought I should have been on the road recruiting, but I wanted to meet the kids on the team. One question I asked them was, "If you could change one thing about Purdue football, or Purdue, what would you change?" From a philosophical point of view, I wanted them to express their attitudes toward Purdue. First-year guys didn't have much to say, but fourth-year guys were pretty insightful.

There were a couple of main themes. Many of them said they wished the students had an interest in football. Some of our minority players talked about how they wished there was more diversity on our campus and in our community. Some things you could do something about, and some things you couldn't.

Some players said they thought Purdue was a basketball school and that nobody cared about football. That prompted us, as the coaches, to do some things during spring football to try to get the students involved. We tried to let everybody know that we would like our

Answering questions from the media with Purdue athletic director Morgan Burke after being introduced as the Boilermakers' head coach. Photo provided courtesy of Purdue University Sports Information

student body to take ownership of the program—knowing full well that just because you sit down and have dinner with them doesn't mean you're going to get results. You've got to give them more than that.

My question to the players was, "What have you guys done that would merit one's confidence in you, that would merit one's support of you?" That got them thinking about their commitment to the program. I had sensed that the players felt a very shallow commitment to the football program, which is why I believed the most important recruits we had in 1997 were the guys who were currently on the roster.

When we took the job in November, we had defensive ends coach Randy Melvin and offensive line coach Jim Chaney—two of our assistants at Wyoming—resign early at Wyoming to sign at Purdue. Melvin was from the Midwest, and Chaney knew the California junior colleges inside and out, so, while the rest of us were busy coaching Wyoming in the playoff game, they went to work recruiting for Purdue.

Once we knew that we were coming to Purdue, the very first thing I did was to return to Wyoming to talk to those coaches, offering the entire staff the opportunity to come to Purdue. Morgan suggested that I might want to keep a coach or two from Colletto's staff, but I told him that I couldn't take the job under those conditions. The assistants at Wyoming were good enough coaches for us to win there; and they'd been loyal, so why wouldn't they be good enough to coach and win at Purdue? I believed that my first loyalty was to the staff at Wyoming. They were the coaches who put us in position to win 10 games and to receive job offers.

I was very upfront with the previous Purdue staff. I told them, before I returned to Wyoming, what I was going to do. After Purdue let us go in 1986, the incoming coach granted interviews to the entire staff. That coach started with the recruiting coordinator, and he met with him for two hours, taking a lot of notes. He wanted to know where Purdue stood in recruiting. Then he began to work his way through the staff. As it turned out, as the day wore on, the meetings began to shorten up. By the time he got down to the last three coaches—Bill Doba, who now is the head coach at Washington State; Bob Spoo, who has been the head coach at Eastern Illinois for years; and me—we were betting on who would be in there the shortest amount of time. We knew what was happening.

The only three questions posed to me during the interview were:

"Who have you recruited that's currently on the roster?"

"Who are your top three recruits at this time?"

"Where do you feel Purdue is with regard to successfully recruiting those top three guys?"

I thought to myself, "If I ever become a head coach, I'm not going to do that. These guys are professionals; these guys are adults; and they deserve the truth."

So, before I went back to Wyoming to coach that playoff game, I had a meeting with the former Purdue staff. I figured it was best to tell those guys exactly what I was thinking. We met in the staff room, and I told them, "Hey, fellas, I was an assistant coach for a long time, including here at Purdue when the head coach was fired, and I know how this works. When you're not successful, the chances of hanging on are slim to none. And I don't want to create any false hope in anyone's mind."

I asked each of them, "If you were on my staff at Wyoming, would you not appreciate the fact that I would come back and offer you the chance to join me at Purdue—especially if they had been loyal?"

Not all of the Purdue coaches agreed, because they didn't have a job, but I think most of them could see where I was coming from.

I continued to shoot straight with them. "This is the way I would want to be treated, and this is the way I'm treating you guys. I'm not creating any false hopes."

I told them that I had yet to talk to the Wyoming staff and that I didn't know about locking down everybody. I told them there was a possibility that I might come back in a week and interview some of them.

When I went back to Wyoming, everybody on that staff said they wanted to come to Purdue. I think I called Morgan Burke, and he told the guys at Purdue that they probably didn't have a job anymore. When we returned to Purdue after that playoff game, we discovered that there was some recruiting information missing, which was disappointing but not a surprise. If you are a jilted lover, so to speak, it's not uncommon for you to tear up the picture of your lover. There were some very good coaches on that staff—and I'm not about to accuse anybody—but somewhere in the transition, a lot of the information on Purdue's recruits came up missing. So maybe I was the greater fool. Maybe I should have done what the previous coach at Purdue had done to us when we were fired. Perhaps I should have collected all the recruiting information and then dropped the bomb.

I just don't operate that way.

When we came to Purdue for good, after the playoff game, we tried to pick up the pieces. Jim and Randy had determined that we were going to have to start from square one in about 80 percent of the cases—and, man, that was coming from a long way back. That was December 11, and we were just now arriving as a staff to begin recruiting, and then I took a week to interview the team.

As it turned out, after the playoff game, Wyoming alum Mike Van Diest decided he was going to stay at his alma mater. Mike has since gone on to become the head coach at Carroll College in Montana and has won three NAIA national championships.

So eight of the nine guys—Chaney, Melvin, Tim Burke, Scott Downing, Danny Hope, Larry Korpitz, Tim Lappano, and Brock Spack—came to Purdue. We added Gary Emanuel, who came highly recommended and proved to be everything we thought he would be. Apart from the favorable schedule and the spread offense, another reason for our early success at Purdue was that we came as a staff and hit the ground running. From top to bottom, it might have been the strongest staff we've had in all the years we've been at Purdue.

"Joe's experience as director of player personnel with Calgary makes him one of the better coaches in the United States. He's a guy who focuses on what he has instead of what he doesn't have. He's positive, and he's competitive. Purdue was a program that people didn't think we could get moving, but Joe got it moving.

"I never had to worry about Joe Tiller doing something that would be inappropriate. He's a man of integrity. If you are square with Joe Tiller, he'll be square with you. If you make a mistake—unless it's really serious—you'll get that one extra chance. You know that you're gone if you do it again. Once you get in his doghouse, it's tough to get out. He's not complicated. If he knows you're putting out, he'll do anything for you."

Morgan Burke

Chapter 9

CHRISTMAS EVERY WEEK

We got such a late start at Purdue that our first recruiting class was ranked No. 11 in the Big Ten by some of the recruiting gurus. But there turned out to be some very solid players in that class, with Drew Brees, of course, being the headliner.

Other players we signed that year included: Akin Ayodele, who went on to the NFL; Chris Clopton, a mini-midget who later started in the Rose Bowl; Jason Loerzel, who started for three years at linebacker; Tim Stratton, who as a senior was awarded the first-ever John Mackey Award as the nation's best tight end; and wide receiver Vinny Sutherland, who made the bubble screen famous. We signed four junior college players in that class as well—Gabe Cox, Billy Gustin, Aaron Starnes, and Henry Bell—and all of them ended up starting for us at one time or another.

It was a rather interesting class, in the sense that even though some had it ranked last in the Big Ten that year, it really turned out to be one of the better recruiting classes we have had. Some fine football players were in that class—guys who ultimately went on to play in the Rose Bowl for us. Of those kids we signed, perhaps two were on

Purdue's list before we arrived. We couldn't believe how many kids had committed elsewhere when we finally began our recruiting push in mid-December. We were really scrambling, mainly trying to find speed. Even though we knew what we were looking for, it was no easy task.

Drew Brees was the only prospect that we chased at both Wyoming and Purdue. Of course, he had told us he wasn't interested in Wyoming. Embarrassing to admit, we nearly forgot about Drew. Not totally, but we sort of put him on the back burner because he had turned us down at Wyoming, and we thought he was saying no to us. He was really saying no to Wyoming and the WAC because he wanted to play at a higher level. In the end, it came down to Kentucky and Purdue—the only two offers that he seriously considered. In terms of dynamite offers from elite programs, few were coming his way.

Once we were at Purdue, his high school coach told us that Drew wasn't interested in playing in the WAC. But now that we were in the Big Ten, his interest rose. Obviously, he was most likely going to have to leave his home state of Texas, because the Big Two—Texas and Texas A&M—did not offer him scholarships. Had we not talked with his coach, who knows what we would have done in terms of recruiting Drew Brees?

We were genuinely excited to get Brees. Hal Mumme was recruiting him at Kentucky, and they were throwing the snot out of the ball. We just felt like Drew was a good bet for us. He was kind of a skinny kid, and we didn't know how good he was, but we thought he had great accuracy and would fit in our system. Our emphasis is really more about accuracy than it is about arm strength. The rest of the world didn't know it at the time, but we knew we were going to throw a lot of swing passes, bubble screens, option routes, and underneath routes—that we really weren't going to throw the ball vertically very often. We were looking for accuracy, competitiveness, and intelligence

A publicity shot of Drew Brees reflecting in my sunglasses. I really don't wear sunglasses, however.
Photo provided courtesy of the Journal-Courier (Lafayette, Indiana)

at the position, and Drew had all those ingredients. We knew we had signed a great guy.

Tim Stratton was a wide receiver with great hands. We thought, "If we could red-shirt him and make him a tight end, he'd have a chance to be a contributor." We knew we had some kids in that class who could run, even though it wasn't a real physical class. We knew Sutherland could really run. On signing day, my thinking was that, if half of the 22 recruits we signed proved to be players, we were probably ahead of the game. We knew we were bringing in some kids who could help us, but we didn't think it was a great class from top to bottom. Under the conditions, we were thrilled to land some of those guys.

Our intention was to use the same winter program that we used at Wyoming. Our 6 a.m. conditioning drills were a real revelation. The

Purdue players had never experienced anything like it. It was challenging, both physically and mentally. They then couldn't believe it when we went from two days a week to three days a week and were shocked when we went from three days to four. Some players were walking, rather than running. They just couldn't keep up, and we wondered if some of them would ever contribute in our program.

Yet, as the years went by, those same guys—I don't want to single anyone out, but his initials begin with Chukky Okobi, continued to make progress and get tougher. Our first year at Purdue, Chukky could not complete the winter conditioning run. By the time he left—and was drafted by the Pittsburgh Steelers—he was leading the offensive linemen in that run even though he weighed more. So, obviously, it was a matter of the right kind of conditioning and his becoming tougher mentally.

We lost a number of players during winter conditioning that first year. The program isn't designed to eliminate anyone. Actually, it's designed to keep everyone in the program, but you try to get them to do things they wouldn't do on their own. One of my favorite quotes is, "No one knows what's in them until they try—and many would never try if they weren't forced to try."

Spring practice was an introduction to a new offense and a new defensive system. We were very unimpressed with our team in the spring. So much so that, after working with the Purdue players on the field, our staff thought we had left a better team behind in Wyoming than the one we had here at a Big Ten school. I still believe that was true.

> "When we came to Purdue, I said that I was not looking forward to having to get used to losing again. Every game you went to you expected to lose, because it was too good to be true. That year nobody went in believing that you were actually going to win."
>
> Arnette Tiller

But we did have some very good players at Purdue, such as Rosevelt Colvin and Chike Okeafor—and one of my all-time favorite Boilermaker players, Mark Fischer. Mark was on that first team, and I loved him. He was an Ohio guy and a tough nut. He just epitomized what I thought a Big Ten offensive lineman should be. He was a good person, a fifth-year senior who really bought into what we were doing. Coach Colletto and his staff did leave some good players behind. Many people wanted to believe that the cupboard was bare, but it wasn't. Golly, Edwin Watson and Kendall Matthews at running back? You mean to tell me the cupboard's bare with those two guys?

We came out of the spring with John Reeves as our starting quarterback. When we went to the Big Ten Kickoff Luncheon in Chicago that summer, John was one of the players we took with us. At the luncheon, after all the media interviews, they held a drawing. The fan with the lucky number had to stand up, and one of the players would throw him a pass. They brought about four or five quarterbacks down front. They tossed John a football, and he was supposed to throw it to a guy who was about three-quarters of the way back in the ballroom—and John's pass didn't even hit the right table. All summer, I kept teasing him about how he lost his starting job at that luncheon. Ironically, we came back from that luncheon, went into two-a-days, and, by the time we opened the season, Billy Dicken was our starting quarterback.

That summer we lost a very good friend and quarterback coach when Larry Korpitz passed away. He had developed a brain tumor, and it was pressing on the part of his brain that affected his memory and his speech. He actually stopped coaching during spring practice. The tumor had been growing for a couple of years. The season before, at Wyoming, we were at a Friday night offensive team meeting, reviewing the game plan. Larry was standing in front of the offensive team, and no words came out. We knew something was wrong, and he was embarrassed. Jim Chaney jumped up, took him by the arm, led him into another room; and I took over the meeting. But he took his medication and came back. At that time, we didn't think it was necessarily life-threatening.

After accepting the Purdue job, I told Larry that I thought he should stay at Wyoming—and he about came out of his chair and attacked me. Here was a guy who I considered one of my very best friends, and he was really upset that I was telling him to stay. I suggested that because of the team of doctors that was treating him. I thought because of family, the health plan, and the location that it was best. He almost became unglued.

"Are you kidding me?" he yelled. "I grew up in Chicago, went to Brother Rice High School—in the heart of Big Ten country. My family lives in Chicago. I get a chance to coach in the Big Ten, and you're telling me I'm not. That's bullshit."

Obviously, he was extremely passionate about going to Purdue and coaching in the Big Ten.

"Okay, I'd love to have you as a coach," I finally relented. "I wasn't talking to you as a coach, I was talking to you as a friend."

Larry had some memory issues. One time he missed a plane, so I became a little leery about putting him on the road, so towards the tail end of recruiting, I had him stay in town. His family had decided to stay in Laramie until the school year was out, but Larry would fly back periodically to visit them, coordinating those trips with his treatments in Boulder, Colorado. Larry's lovely wife, Jo, made Coach Chaney, who was very close to Larry, promise he would let her know if her husband really began to slide.

Larry was staying in an apartment, and, one time during spring football, he was convinced he had forgotten his clothes at the laundromat. But they couldn't find them, so they thought somebody had stolen his clothes. The next day, Larry opened his closet and there were all his clothes in a hamper—he had never gone to the laundromat. Coach Chaney called Jo, and she flew to Purdue for the weekend. She asked me what I thought about Larry.

"I think he should go home," I told her. "He needs to be home around his kids. We can make it through spring practice without him."

Jo said she was hoping I would say that, so he went back to Wyoming.

Later that spring, we received word that his health was continuing to fail. They planned a weekend for all of Larry's friends to gather at the house back in Laramie. Jim and I went, planning to drink beer, barbeque, tell lies, and laugh. There were a number of his high school and college friends there. Larry was wearing sweats, and he was very tired. He visited a little bit, but then he excused himself and went to lie down. We stayed for a couple hours, but Larry never came back out while we were there. Coach Chaney and I both knew that would be the last time we would see our friend. Sure enough, in July, Arnette and I flew back West for his funeral.

Larry's replacement was a 34-year-old whippersnapper named Greg Olson, who had been a graduate assistant for us at Washington State in 1989 and 1990. We knew him, and, more importantly, we trusted him. I've always preferred to hire someone I've worked with previously, and Greg did a great job for us.

We opened that 1997 season, and our tenure at Purdue, in the Glass Bowl in Toledo. We were very underwhelming in a 36-22 loss— in my own hometown, which was very embarrassing. I had cousins, nieces and nephews, aunts and uncles, who—for years and years and years—had never seen me play or coach a game. I had about 40 relatives and friends at that game. They were doing the tailgate bit and everything. All those people were there to see Big Joey coach a game— and we proceeded to get spanked by the Rockets. The turning point in the game may have been *before* the kickoff, when the public address announcer introduced me as, "Jim Tiller, an old Toledo hero."

I thought, "Holy Toledo, what did we get ourselves into?"

> "Before our first game at Toledo, Joe's hometown, they introduced him as 'Jim Tiller.' After we lost that game, with 8,000 Tillers there, Assistant Coach Danny Hope came out of the locker room, and his tie was kind of crooked. I gave him a hug and straightened his tie. He looked at me and said, 'Tried to hang myself ... the rope broke.'
> Arnette Tiller

In the staff room the next day, I asked the other coaches, "How can we get all those guys at Wyoming to transfer to Purdue so we can get better quickly?"

But the next week we beat Notre Dame 28-17 at home, which I knew was big; but I didn't really know how big until after it happened. The fans in Ross-Ade Stadium erupted when we threw the ball on third-and-one. They were used to watching Mike Alstott run the ball, and that was a glimpse of the future at Purdue. To show the players that all our hard work had a purpose was significant, too.

After that, we went on a roll, winning six in a row, and things were looking good until we went to Iowa, and the Hawkeyes knocked us into tomorrow, 35-17. Iowa dominated us physically, and I didn't see too many of our guys—even the ones we considered to be our better players—jumping to the front of the line to get a piece of the action. They were simply docile.

We played Penn State at home the following week and got a repeat of the Iowa game. The Nittany Lions had Curtis Enis, who had thighs bigger than my waist. He destroyed us, rushing 37 times for 186 yards and four touchdowns. Physically, they grabbed hold of us and beat us like rag dolls. After the game, I wanted to go up to Enis and say, "Son, you're a great player; and you're wasting your time at the collegiate level." He was a junior, and I wanted to encourage him to move on—but I didn't, of course.

As that first season unfolded, I enjoyed the fact that no one painted a scenario a month in advance: "If they do this and this, they'll go to this bowl; if they do this and that, they'll go to that bowl; if they don't go to this or that bowl, it's going to be very disappointing." None of that took place that first year. We didn't start the season with the thought of going bowling, and I don't think any media—particularly after that Toledo loss—thought we would end up in a bowl game. It never entered their minds. That maybe was the purest football season I've ever experienced.

A few days after the season, athletic director Morgan Burke called and said, "Congratulations, you're going to San Antonio." I had to think for a second, "Which bowl game was in San Antonio?" I didn't have any expectation of going to any particular bowl. I knew we were going to go somewhere, but I had no idea where. It didn't hit me until a day later that, although we had a better record than Wisconsin and had beaten them 45-20 during the season, the Badgers were going to the Outback Bowl, and we were going to the Alamo Bowl—third and fourth, respectively, in the Big Ten's bowl pecking order.

The Alamo Bowl, though, turned out to be a great experience. Of all the bowls I've been to—I'm not going to say any one is my favorite—but it would be one of my top three. Because of the Riverwalk in San Antonio, it has the best interaction of any bowl. You see fans of the opposing team all week long, not just on game day. You sit in the same restaurants with them, sing fight songs with them. It's good, clean fun—a weeklong festival. The atmosphere in San Antonio is very difficult to beat. We played Oklahoma State in the bowl game, and we were really concerned about their speed; but they couldn't figure out our offense, and we won, 33-20.

That first season at Purdue was definitely one to remember. After the victory over Notre Dame, Arnette planned a party. She invited neighbors, old friends, the coaching staff, and their families. We must have had 80 people at the house after that game. Somebody bought some cigars, and we went out on the deck to smoke and enjoy the victory. I was thinking, "Hey, this is a pretty good life." That became somewhat of a tradition with us. We'd smoke a victory cigar after every win. None of us really smoked cigars. Matter of fact, after a dozen puffs, I've about had it with one of them.

After the Wisconsin game, which was Homecoming, we didn't have any recruits in, so we went to a restaurant in downtown Lafayette and spent the evening with friends. We didn't have a single official visit during the season. We were operating under the same premise we did at Wyoming, that you really didn't start recruiting until after the season. We weren't aware of the changing landscape in recruiting, especially in the Big Ten and other major conferences—that more and more recruiting was taking place during the season.

Signing autographs in assembly-line fashion at the Alamo Bowl.
Photo provided courtesy of the Journal-Courier (Lafayette, Indiana)

After a victory at Indiana, our eighth of the season, we came back to our place and had pizza delivered. As a staff, we spent time with each other in a social environment. You can't do that today, with the advent of in-season recruiting. That's one of the things I miss—the camaraderie with the staff. After a game now, you have to put on a happy face and entertain recruits. You have to spend the evening with your very latest, newest, best friends. That's not my idea of enjoying the benefits of a week's labor.

Not only was 1997 a fun season on the field, it was fun afterward. The staff got to spend time with our family and friends. We were more like fans after the game than coaches. That year was clearly the most enjoyable I've ever had as a coach.

When you put the whole package together, '97 was Christmas every week—just go home after the game and open up a present ... open that box of cigars.

Chapter 10

THE PRESSURE BUILDS

Following that incredible 1997 season, Boilermaker fans were very giddy. Everybody wanted to know how winning nine games and going to a bowl game would help us in recruiting. What we found out was, going to one bowl game had next to no impact in that area. We tried to elevate our recruiting and zero in on higher profile recruits, but the schools we were competing against had all been to multiple bowl games. Most people, including the media, assumed that this bowl thing was some big windfall—that suddenly we were going to go from having the No. 11 recruiting class in the Big Ten to No. 1. Recruiting that next season was my first tip that expectations didn't necessarily fall in line with reality at Purdue.

We made some mistakes recruiting that second year at Purdue. We signed seven junior college kids, which is too many, and we signed too many Indiana kids. We took too many in-state recruits who were developmental kids, and only one of seven ended up making it. That almost proved fatal, but we were able to recover over the next couple of years. That 1998 recruiting class was ranked higher—as high as third in the Big Ten—but I'm sure it wasn't justified. I think they did it because we were the new story, the new hot program. Another example of how, oftentimes, the media doesn't get it.

During our first season at Purdue, the staff did a great job of coaching, and our players did a great job of playing; so some group out of Detroit picked me as the coach of the year. The awards banquet was held in the incredible Fox Theatre. Michigan coach Lloyd Carr, whose team shared the national championship with Nebraska in 1997 and featured the Heisman Trophy winner in Charles Woodson, spoke about the difference between a good year and a great year. Coach Carr said, "In order to have a great season, you need to have some young players step up that you don't expect to do so."

I would agree with that, because the year we went to the Rose Bowl was the year that Stuart Schweigert came on board—and we didn't give up a single home run that year. Every season, we had been giving up long plays, such as a 60-yard run for a touchdown. But Schweigert, although he was only 18 years old and not real physical, was a great open-field tackler—and he had the speed to get there.

Before the awards ceremony, Arnette and I were in our hotel room getting dressed. I had put on my tuxedo and was standing in front of the mirror, when I said, "Well dear, how many great football coaches do you think are out there?" She looked at me and said, "One less than you think." She brought me down to earth in a heartbeat.

One of the positive things heading into the 1998 season was that the players who were coming back knew what the winter workouts were all about—and they had enjoyed some success, so they were willing to put more into them. That year was a turn-the-corner year for us in terms of commitment. Guys really got with it.

Our coaching staff changed a little bit. Jim Chaney became the offensive coordinator, and we lost Tim Lappano to the NFL. He couldn't resist joining his former coach, Dennis Erickson, who had just become the head coach of the Seattle Seahawks. We replaced Tim with a former Purdue player, Kevin Sumlin, who came in to coach our wide receivers. He had been at Minnesota and was familiar with the Big Ten. A very significant change was when we were able to hire Jim Lathrop as our strength coach. He had done a great job for us at Wyoming, and he wanted to come to Purdue with us in '97, but it wasn't doable at that time. Jim is one of our key employees. He was a critical hire at that time and has continued to have a major impact on our program.

During the spring game that year, Drew Brees had to play for both teams, because we were short-handed at quarterback. The most impressive thing about that game was that his arm remained attached to his shoulder. We liked many of the things Drew was doing, but we really didn't know how good he was going to be, and that's why we recruited David Edgerton, a junior-college quarterback. We knew that we had a guy who would be able to do some of the things we wanted and do them well, but we didn't really know how special a talent Drew ultimately would become.

> "Guys who didn't buy into what Coach Tiller was trying to do? They were out of there. If you weren't buying in, you couldn't help us win, and therefore you shouldn't be there. We were a disciplined team. We did things the right way. If you didn't, you were punished. If you didn't go to class, if you were late for meetings or late for practice, you were punished. That doesn't mean you couldn't have fun. I can definitely say we did a lot of that. But in order to have real fun, you have to win. They kind of go together."
>
> Drew Brees

As the season drew near, Morgan Burke approached me about playing an early-season game. At that time, a number of those games existed, and the idea intrigued me until I heard what they had in mind—the only games offered to Purdue were on the road.

I think the Kickoff Classic came at us first, wanting us to play at Florida State. That didn't really interest me. I didn't think we wanted to put our team in that type of environment, particularly with a first-year quarterback. Then the Pigskin Classic approached us with a Sunday afternoon game against Southern California in the Los Angeles Coliseum. That was just too good an offer to turn down. At that time, Paul Hackett was coaching USC, and Carson Palmer was the quarterback. They had a good team, but they weren't a national juggernaut yet. Florida State was a national juggernaut—USC was a national player.

The Pigskin Classic actually netted the university more dollars than a bowl game—a total of about $600,000—because we just took our coaches, team, and immediate support staff. We didn't take the band. We weren't at the site very long, and we didn't have to share the money with the rest of the Big Ten. At that time, we had only one outdoor practice field, which wasn't in very good shape. So the athletic director dangled a carrot in front of the football coach and said, "If you guys will play in the Pigskin Classic, we'll take some of the revenue and build another outdoor practice field." I felt that would make us a better program, especially since I never was interested in practicing indoors.

While we were in Los Angeles, I planned our schedule so we would have enough time to take a side trip to the Rose Bowl. I wanted our players to walk the field and to visualize playing there. We took a team photo on the field at the Rose Bowl and posted it in our locker room for motivation.

We lost 27-17 to Southern Cal in a very competitive game, and Brees made an incredible play in the fourth quarter. We were in the red zone and had called a pass. Brees had to step up in the pocket, jump to his right to avoid a rush, and then sidearm the ball out of there. He put it right on a receiver's chest at the goal line. I looked at our guys on the sideline and said, "Wow, we've got ourselves a quarterback."

The weather was terrible for that game. The temperature was in the 90s, but the killer was the intense humidity. When we went up the tunnel to the locker room at halftime, gurneys stretched along the wall holding USC band members, who were dropping like flies in the heat. It was stifling, especially on the floor of the Coliseum, where the air couldn't get to you. That game really was the ultimate challenge.

Our second game was against Rice, and I was worried because they were a wishbone team. When we were at Wyoming and played Air Force, another wishbone team, it seemed as if somebody's ankle would get crushed, or some other type of leg injury would occur because of the blocking scheme used in that offense. Sure enough, our starting defensive tackle, Brent Botts, broke an ankle against Rice and didn't play the rest of the season.

Central Florida was next, and I was anxious to see this giant phenom of a quarterback they had by the name of Daunte Culpepper. He proved to be everything he was billed to be. He treated a couple of our defensive linemen like shoo flies. They'd try to tackle him, and he'd knock them out of the way with a stiff-arm, step up, and throw the ball.

The turning point of that season was our 31-13 loss at Penn State, which was on a roll at that time. As I walked off the field at Beaver Stadium, I had to wonder how far we were from the better teams in the league. Not having played Ohio State or Michigan since I took over, I began to question how we really stacked up in the Big Ten.

But we came back from that game to win our last five regular-season games and finish 8-4, 6-2 in the Big Ten. I was convinced we were going to a Florida bowl game to play on New Year's Day, either in the Capital One Bowl or the Outback Bowl, so I was shocked when we found out that we were returning to the Alamo Bowl. That was the first time I sensed disappointment in the Purdue people. The previous year, everybody was just so giddy it didn't matter what happened. In 1998, it was almost the same thing, but everybody was convinced that we were going to Florida. I was hesitant about returning to the Alamo Bowl. Since we weren't going somewhere new, would we still have a good time? Would the players be bored? But as it turned out, everything was better the second time around. Fortunately, we had a good experience at the Alamo Bowl the year before, so many people made the repeat trip. When it was all said

After Purdue's first bowl victory in 17 years, the players provided me with a last-minute shower.
Photo provided courtesy of the Journal-Courier (Lafayette, Indiana)

and done, our numbers were improved over the previous year. I actually think our team and our fans had a better time at the second Alamo Bowl.

We were shocked to find out that our opponent was Kansas State. The Wildcats had been ranked No. 1 in the country until they lost to Texas A&M in the Big 12 Conference title game. Still, here we were, going to the Alamo Bowl to play the fourth-ranked team in the country. Winning 37-34 in the final seconds topped off what became an almost-perfect bowl trip. During my entire coaching career, I don't recall so many people commenting about how much fun they had after a game. Even after the Rose Bowl, people still refer to that second Alamo Bowl.

Of all the games I've coached, that one ranks awfully high because we were a huge underdog, and we beat a great team. It was an unbelievable comeback. We lost a 14-point lead in the fourth quarter, but

Accepting the Alamo Bowl Championship Trophy in 1997. We've always tried to let the players have the spotlight. Photo provided courtesy of Purdue University Sports Information

with Kansas State leading, 34-30, Brees drove us 80 yards in only 54 seconds to score the winning touchdown with just 30 seconds remaining—a perfect 24-yard pass just over a defender's shoulder to Isaac Jones, who made a fantastic catch. We won that game with a sophomore quarterback, so the future looked very good. Football was alive and well at Purdue at that time—so much so that the athletic director offered me a new contract.

Reflecting back, that 1998 season ended the pure fun at Purdue. As I said, that first season was like Christmas every week, and the second year was very similar. After that season, that great appreciation Purdue people showed us changed to great expectations.

The question was no longer, "Do you think we can go to a bowl game?"

Suddenly, people were asking, "When are we going to the Rose Bowl?"

I think that's natural, but I don't think that you should ever forget your roots—and I think many Purdue people totally forgot our roots. In recruiting, people wanted to know if we were going to steal this kid away from Ohio State or take that guy away from Michigan. Two years earlier, we were worried about trying to beat Ipswich Tech for a kid.

As much as you wanted everything to stay genuine, so to speak, the pressure began to mount. For a coach to have a stress-free season is a rare opportunity—no baggage from past seasons, unrealistic expectations, or talk about how much is enough—and we were lucky to have two such seasons at Purdue.

Chapter 11

A TOUGH WEEK IN TAMPA

We actually had a better team in 1998 than we had in 1999, but in '99 we were selected to go to the Outback Bowl in Tampa—finally making it to our first New Year's Day bowl. Strangely, that selection alleviated pressure while adding even more. All of a sudden people were saying, "What the heck? We made it to a New Year's Day bowl, so when are we going to the Rose Bowl?" Again, I think you can't lose sight of who you are and where you came from, because it's very difficult—within the Purdue culture—to improve dramatically in a short period of time.

Maybe the 1999 season was soured by the tough week we had in Tampa. Ybor City—the Latin Quarter section of Tampa, with bars, nightclubs, and restaurants—turned out to be too much of an attraction for some of our players, and I had to send a couple home. I couldn't help but think, "If this is what New Year's Day does for you, let's go back to the Alamo Bowl—or let's go to some other bowl game that's more fun."

I'd never experienced such a miserable bowl week. Fortunately, we haven't had a repeat of that.

We had a number of Florida players on our roster, and they were all jacked up about going back home. It was as if we weren't there to play a football game, we were there just to stay up 24 hours a day to soak in the Florida sunshine and to take in all the activities and parties of a New Year's Day bowl. Then the game itself was very disappointing because we jumped out to a 25-0 lead over Georgia early in the second quarter but ended up losing, 28-25, in overtime. Who knows—maybe we didn't have enough gas at the end of that game simply because of the way we carried on that week. That was a tough week on the coaching staff; it was a tough week on me. Having to send players home is never any fun.

I really didn't like the fact that we changed as the expectation level changed at Purdue. We were pretty ironfisted when we first showed up, and we didn't tolerate any nonsense. In '99, the old Joe Tiller probably would have sent home about a dozen players. I could have very easily sent home eight or nine starters. The reason I didn't was, I felt we couldn't field a representative team without them, and I didn't think that would be fair to the rest of the players—the guys who were behaving themselves and taking care of business. I asked

"Near the end of the fall semester of my sophomore season, a bunch of guys on the team had lied to coach Tiller about their grades and they ended up in some academic trouble.

"So a couple of weeks into the spring semester, Coach Tiller held a team meeting. He walked into the room with a real somber look, went up to the podium, and said, 'I want you guys to hear this from me before it gets out. I've taken the head coaching job at the University of Colorado, and I'm taking the entire staff with me. It's been a pleasure coaching you. I know this is probably a shock to you, but I've made my decision. I wish you the best of luck.'

"And then he walked out of the room. It was very quick–probably only about two minutes, and he was out of the room. We had just come off this huge victory over Kansas State, we felt that the program was going in the right direction. Coach Tiller is leaving? We were absolutely shocked, upset, disappointed, and borderline mad.

"A couple minutes later, Coach Tiller came back into the room and said, 'Just kidding. I just wanted you guys to know what it felt like to be lied to. Some of you guys lied about your grades last semester and got yourselves in academic trouble, which put the team in a compromising position. It's not very much fun to be lied to, is it? I'm still your coach; but make sure you tell the truth and do what you're supposed to and do it the right way.'

"It's hilarious looking back, but Coach Tiller got the message across."

Drew Brees

myself, "If I send all those guys home, am I eliminating the good guys' opportunities to be successful?" That was, and is, always a part of the equation. Canning a guy is easy—turning a negative into a positive without unjustly punishing the good kids, though, is very difficult.

I also didn't like the fact that I allowed outside influences to impact my decision—with it being our first Florida bowl game and our first New Year's Day bowl game, and with so many Purdue fans and alums there. Maybe I shouldn't, but I think about those things. I feel obligated to our fan base. If they're there, we should make sure we hold up our end of the bargain, to the best of our ability, as coaches and players.

That game was the last time I used the chart that tells coaches whether to go for an extra point or a two-point conversion after a touchdown. Like most coaches, I had used the chart for years and had become a believer in it. In that game, though, I learned that football is not all about mathematics or statistics. Mathematicians—who don't factor in the human element—created the chart, but the game is played by humans.

Against Georgia, after we missed an extra point following our second touchdown, we decided to try two-point conversions after our next two TDs—but we were unsuccessful each time. We made that decision, of course, because that's what the chart indicated. The Bulldogs ended up scoring a touchdown with just over a minute to play in regulation to tie it and then kicked a 21-yard field goal to win the game in overtime.

That prompted me to talk to as many coaches around the country as I could during the off-season, gathering their thoughts on the when, how, and why behind each point-after decision. From that day on, I changed my philosophy, and we no longer have a chart. One thing's for sure—I'm never again going for two in the first half, period. There's too much football to be played, so forget the mathematical formulas.

One of the things I remember most about that season was getting thumped 38-12 at Michigan. They were ranked No. 4 in the country,

At the postgame press conference at the 2000 Outback Bowl, I couldn't wait to get out of there and head back home. Photo provided courtesy of Purdue University Sports Information

and it was the first time we had played them since we arrived at Purdue. I thought we had a heck of a plan, and I really thought we were ready to play. We didn't drop a single pass during our pregame warmups. We probably threw 40 or 50 passes during our pregame drills, and everybody caught everything. I thought, "Man, this team is really dialed in."

Then the game began, and I think we dropped six of our first seven passes. We lost big, and something happened after that game that spoke volumes about those increased expectations that were creeping into the program. During my postgame interview, I said, "Overall, they're a better football team than we are. We always talk about leaving the game on the field, but today I thought we brought a lot of our game back into our locker room. In a game like this, you should be exhausted."

That was the truth, but I got criticized for saying that. Fans called in, saying, "Coach, you don't think we're as good as Michigan?" My response was, "Hell, no." The audacity to suggest that we were at that level after only two years in the program was insane. The media, of course, fueled the critics once again.

The next week, we lost a 25-22 heartbreaker at Ohio State, which was ranked No. 21—despite the fact that we finished with more total yards, we didn't throw any interceptions, and we controlled the time of possession. After the game, I told the media, "This certainly isn't as tough to take as the Michigan loss, because the effort was better."

After beating No. 5 Michigan State 52-28—even though the Spartans scored two defensive touchdowns on long interception returns—we were defeated at home, 31-25, by a very good Penn State team that was No. 2 in the country. A great game, but the Nittany Lions' two defensive studs killed us. Linebacker LaVar Arrington returned a fumble two yards for a touchdown, and defensive end Courtney Brown batted a pass up in the air for an interception that he returned 25 yards for another score. Penn State's two superstars showed up big in that game. A common theme exists on every great team—you can count on your "go-to" guys to perform at their best in the toughest situation

As it turned out, 1999 was a decent season. We finished 7-5 overall and 4-4 in the Big Ten, but, after we began the season with four consecutive victories, that was a little disappointing. Some of the seniors, who, I guess for the lack of a better term, were jealous of Drew Brees, was another reason why that season was not as much fun. They felt like, "We're seniors—we've been here for four or five years. And the cameras are focused on this junior quarterback?" Resentment surfaced—not team-wide—amongst three or four seniors, a couple of whom approached me about the publicity they were receiving versus the publicity Brees was receiving. They thought they should be getting

I'm either trying to fire up the Boilermakers or voicing displeasure at the officiating.
Photo provided courtesy of Purdue University Sports Information

a bigger piece of the pie. They all really liked Drew—that wasn't the problem—but they felt slighted.

Things like that were creeping in. We didn't have any of that in '97 or '98, so all of a sudden, it wasn't as much fun. It wasn't agenda-free. Things started losing some of their flavor—and more and more outsiders were beginning to weigh in with their opinions and their viewpoints.

Some may say that's better than being ignored, but I'm not 100 percent sure that's true.

Chapter 12

CALIFORNIA, HERE WE COME

After the 1999 season, there was a lot of concern surrounding the Purdue program because Drew Brees was considering skipping his senior year and declaring for the NFL Draft. He had put together two consecutive outstanding seasons. As a sophomore in 1998, he set Big Ten records with 3,983 yards passing and 39 touchdown passes. In 1999, he passed for 3,909 yards and 25 touchdowns—all while cutting his interceptions from 20 in '98 to 12 in '99. As a junior, Drew finished fourth in the Heisman Trophy balloting behind Wisconsin running back Ron Dayne and quarterbacks Joe Hamilton of Georgia Tech and Michael Vick of Virginia Tech. Brees was also runner-up in the voting for the Davey O'Brien National Quarterback Award (Hamilton) and the Maxwell Award as the nation's top player (Dayne).

In talking to Drew and his family about investigating the NFL, I felt like they trusted me. I don't think I talked him into coming back—I think he talked himself into coming back. I just presented the facts, as I understood them: he really could improve himself by coming back and playing his senior season. I talked to three of the top front-office people in the NFL—Bill Polian, Bobby Beathard, and Ron Wolfe—and they all agreed that Drew needed to come back. They all agreed that he was probably a third- or fourth-rounder, but he could play his way into a higher round, and that's exactly what happened.

Everybody was on pins and needles on the day of his press conference. When he finally announced that he was going to play his senior season at Purdue, I told the media, "I need to go to the hospital to get this grin removed from my face."

Heading into that 2000 season, we had a lot of promise, the expectations were very high, and we were receiving a lot of national publicity. Drew handled everything very well. He and Jim Vruggink, then Purdue's sports information director, developed a great relationship and really worked hard at coming up with ways of effectively marketing Drew.

Without a doubt, Brees was a marquee player. Before the season even started, 10 or 11 of our games already were designated as television games. As it turned out, every game was televised—most of them nationally televised. Drew is really the only marquee player we've had in our tenure at Purdue. A couple of other players probably deserved that status, but it never came their way.

Drew may have been the marquee player, but our outstanding offensive line that season probably had just as much to do with our success in 2000. We had Brandon Gorin at right tackle and Matt Light, the best player of the group, at left tackle. Freshman Gene Mruczkowski, who went on to be a four-year starter, played left guard, with Ian Allen at right guard and Chukky Okobi at center. Every one of those guys went on to play on Sundays.

> "I'll never forget his eyebrow lift. He'd be talking to you and, I think, trying to get in your head a little bit with the whole eyebrow thing. After the conversation, you'd be like, 'Wait a minute, what just happened?' He would make me laugh, but at the same time, he would be telling me I needed to get better. Right at the end, he'd give you that eyebrow lift—and he'd give you the wink all the time too. The wink and the double-eyebrow lift were awesome. That let you know he was trying to get a point across."
>
> Drew Brees

In New York at the 2000 Heisman Trophy presentation with (left to right) Arnette, Drew Brees, and Drew's mom, Mina. It was a great experience. Photo provided by the Joe Tiller family

In addition to Brees and an outstanding offensive line, we had Tim Stratton, who won the first-ever John Mackey Award as the best tight end in the nation. He was Mr. Third Down—when we threw it to him he caught it 95 percent of the time. We also had the speedy Vinny Sutherland as an outside wide receiver.

We had several youngsters that year, seven or eight freshmen, who played key roles on our defense. I really began to appreciate Lloyd Carr's comments about newcomers being major contributors. Perhaps the guy who had the biggest impact was Stuart Schweigert, who started at safety and became an outstanding open-field tackler. Gilbert Gardner came to us that year as a wide receiver and safety, but, by the third game of season, he was our starting middle linebacker against

Notre Dame. Craig Terrill started at defensive tackle, Shaun Phillips at defensive end, and Landon Johnson at linebacker—and each had a huge impact on our success, and they all went on to play in the NFL.

We had an early setback when we lost a close one at No. 21 Notre Dame, 23-21, when Nick Setta kicked a 38-yard field goal as time expired. In that game, we had three costly turnovers that led to 17 points for the Fighting Irish—a blocked punt that led to a touchdown, an interception returned for another touchdown, and a failed fake punt attempt that led to a field goal. One of the strangest plays I've ever seen was the fake punt attempt. Notre Dame was leading 17-14 in the third quarter, when Travis Dorsch dropped back to punt on a fourth-and-23 from our 23-yard line. Instead of punting the ball, he tried to throw it to Vinny Sutherland, who wasn't expecting a pass—a play that wasn't called from the sideline. Dorsch said that he audibled to the pass, but no one else heard him change the play. He probably did, but it's always loud in that stadium.

Two games later, we were 3-1 heading to play Penn State at Happy Valley. The Nittany Lions scored off two botched punts deep in our territory, and we lost a heartbreaker, 22-20. Walking off that field, I was extremely disappointed—I thought we had the type of team to go in there and win—and I was really depressed as I walked back to the locker room with Morgan Burke. I told him, "I just don't know if we ever are going to be good enough to win a Big Ten championship."

We came back the following week and beat sixth-ranked Michigan, 32-31, which was a huge help. The Wolverines had committed a holding penalty right before halftime. They were down in the red zone, so we could have declined the penalty; but they would have kicked a field goal. Instead, we took the penalty and backed them up, but they connected on a 15-yard touchdown pass with 13 seconds left to take a 28-10 lead. In the locker room at halftime, I told the team, "Hey, fellas, you've got to believe that you're going to win at all times. We declined that penalty because we believe in you guys. We believed that you would stop them. Your coaches believe in you, so you guys have to believe in your ability to win this game."

I'm not saying that what I said inspired them, but we went out, played a great second half, and won the game. Our defense held Michigan to three points in the final two quarters, and then Travis Dorsch, with a flair for the dramatic, took advantage of a second chance. Dorsch missed a 32-yard field goal with 2:11 remaining but came back to kick a 33-yard game-winner with four seconds left.

The Michigan victory really kick-started us. After beating Northwestern the following week, we went to Wisconsin and won in overtime, 30-24. Craig Terrill blocked a 58-yard field goal attempt, and Ashante Woodyard scooped up the ball and returned it 36 yards for a touchdown.

We were back in the title hunt.

The Ohio State game was a very emotional game and one of the most significant during our tenure at Purdue. Dorsch got a second chance against Michigan, and Brees got a second opportunity against the Buckeyes. After throwing an interception that led to an Ohio State score and a 27-24 lead with 2:16 remaining, Brees came back to deliver a perfect pass to Seth Morales, who slipped behind the OSU secondary, for a 65-yard touchdown that gave us a 31-27 victory.

I distinctly remember standing on our field after the Buckeyes had intercepted Brees. I remember it as if it were yesterday. Drew was scrambling, and, as he was hit, the ball sailed on him and was intercepted. The thought that went through my mind wasn't, "We're going to lose this game." My thought was, "This kid deserves better than this. He's done it all for this program, and he deserves better than this."

He then calmly threw the winning touchdown pass.

We were feeling pretty good about ourselves, but then we went up and got waxed 30-10 at Michigan State. That's the only bad game that Brees had during his years at Purdue. He threw three intercep-

At the Rose Bowl press conference.
Photo provided courtesy of the Journal-Courier (Lafayette, Indiana)

tions and was never sharp the entire game. We thought we had just lost our chance to go to the Rose Bowl, so I wasn't feeling very good coming out of the locker room. Then I got on the team bus outside Spartan Stadium, and one of our coaches heard [on the radio] that Iowa had defeated Northwestern, our chief challenger. Maybe the football gods were smiling on us after all. If we could beat Indiana in the last regular-season game, we would go to the Rose Bowl.

We beat Indiana, 41-13, and one of the most memorable moments of my career took place after that game—watching our coaches, players, and fans celebrate. The field was covered with people, but the stands still seemed full. That was an emotional highlight for me—not so much because of the victory, but because of the significance of that

> "After a victory, Coach Tiller was all smiles in the locker room. Everybody used to say it was 'Tiller Time,' but he'd get up on a box in the locker room, look at us, and say, 'Nice job, boys—now it's Miller Time.' It was always a classic Joe Tiller moment."
>
> Drew Brees

A picture I'll always treasure—with Drew Brees on the field at Ross-Ade Stadium, after clinching the trip to Pasadena. Photo provided courtesy of Purdue University Sports Information

game. The coaches were hugging each other on the field, and I kept saying, "Oh, my God, we're going to the Rose Bowl! Purdue is going to the Rose Bowl!"

Awestruck, I kept thinking, "Who'da thunk it? Here's a kid who grew up on a dead-end street in Toledo, Ohio, and I'm going to coach in the Rose Bowl."

After that night, I didn't think a whole lot more about it because the Rose Bowl was more consuming than any other bowl, with more obligations and more things to do. I've never coached in a bowl game where I've been able to relax. I don't think I've ever gone out to dinner with my family more than once on site at any bowl game. There was always a function to attend.

At the Rose Bowl, I was only able to stop and smell the roses, so to speak, twice. Coming out of the tunnel for pregame warmups, I walked across the corner of the end zone that had *Purdue* painted in gold and black. I stopped for a minute to take that in. And then right before kickoff, I put my headset on, looked around, and thought, "Wow, this is really something—this is really happening."

Besides the game itself, the most impressive thing during the entire week at the Rose Bowl was the pep rally that Purdue staged. Twenty thousand or more Boilermaker fans, maybe more, came to support us. I was flabbergasted. If you didn't realize how big that game was before, that sent the message. That was almost as impressive as the game-day scene.

We had finished the regular season 8-3 and ranked No. 14. Our opponent was No. 4 Washington, which overall had a little better team speed. The big difference was their offensive line versus our defensive line. Their physical superiority was a definite concern for us, and I figured that we had to be at the top of our game to win. We got off to a very poor start and fell behind 14-0. We came back and made it a competitive game, losing 34-24, but afterwards I felt like they were a more physical team than we were. We didn't play our best game, which we needed to do.

Washington was just a better team.

Making it to the Rose Bowl with an 8-3 record, only two losses in the Big Ten, validated my thinking that, in order for Purdue to get to Pasadena, we'd have to have that type of season. Purdue may never be able to run the table—something most Boilermaker fans don't want to fess up to, but that's the reality.

Because of that reality, going to the Rose Bowl was more than special.

We did it—and for only the second time in Purdue football history.

Chapter 13

SUNNY EL PASO

After our tremendous journey to the Rose Bowl in 2000, we realized that we were losing a great talent in Drew Brees. While we believed we had the makings of a respectable team, we weren't misleading ourselves in any way. We knew we wouldn't be as good in 2001 as we were in 2000.

I think I had done a decent job of keeping everything in perspective each year, including after our Rose Bowl season. At Purdue, it's a year-to-year thing. In other words, I don't think you could ever say, "Oh, we've got it made as a program. We're going to be good forever." At Purdue, it's always a real challenge.

The year after we played in the Rose Bowl, I thought that, if we could go to a bowl game despite suffering some tremendous personnel losses, we would demonstrate that we had a program versus just having a team. That was my philosophy for two or three years running. People asked me about the success we had and what it meant, and my response was always, "It meant we had a good team that year, but not necessarily that we had a good program in place."

We suffered staggering personnel losses from the Rose Bowl team. There aren't many programs in the country that could sustain the losses that Purdue did that year and have a winning season. That was what the 2001 season was all about, even though we finished with a mediocre 6-6 record. Brandon Hance began the year as Brees' replacement, and even though we got off to a great start with five victories in our first six games, we recognized that we had some limitations, particularly at the quarterback position. We started working true freshman Kyle Orton into the lineup at midseason, and then Orton started our final three games that year.

Of course, 2001 was the year of the September 11 terrorist attacks. Following those horrible events, we cancelled practice and had a team meeting in our locker room. I told the players that our lives would never be the same. I told them that some of the freedoms we had enjoyed in the past would be gone forever—because this was the first attack ever on our soil. We had a couple players, linebacker Niko Koutouvides and wide receiver Chris James, who had relatives working in the towers; and they were trying to find out about their situations. Fortunately, they were all okay.

The whole nation was in a state of shock, and we weren't any different. For a day, we were like everyone else, just wandering aimlessly, not knowing what to do except to watch the news and check with Niko and Chris to see if they had located their family members. Then there was the question of whether we would play our scheduled game that week against Notre Dame. Earlier that week, Notre Dame officials said they didn't want to play, but since it was a home date for us, we decided we would keep that option open. Whatever college football was going to do, we were going to go along with it. In the end, all of the games nationwide were postponed, which pushed our game with Notre Dame back into December—and that was the right thing to do.

We took a day off and then decided, under the circumstances, the best thing we could do was to get our team back to practice so we could get our minds off 9/11—just to return to some sense of normalcy. However, the practice didn't go very well since no one's mind was on football. Everyone, including the coaches, was just going through the motions.

We were 6-3 heading into our game at Indiana, which normally would have been our final regular-season game. We didn't expect to lose at Indiana, which had the very athletic Antwaan Randle El at quarterback, but we did, 13-7. That game was played in a monsoon-like downpour, and we failed to capitalize on two drives that began in Indiana territory and failed to score when we went for it on a fourth-and-goal from the 1-yard line early in the fourth quarter. One of their guys reached up and, with one hand, tripped up our running back short of the goal line. All I could think was, "I could spit that far."

The Notre Dame game turned out to be an aberration. We finished with 332 yards to 162 for the Fighting Irish. We also outpassed them, 258 yards to 31, picked up 12 more first downs, and had the ball for five more minutes. Yet, we had four turnovers and lost 24-18. That was the best defensive game we had played up to that point at Purdue, but it came in a losing effort.

We were invited to El Paso, Texas, to play in the Sun Bowl against a very good Washington State team, which was a fun bowl since I knew many of the coaches on the Cougars' staff—including one of my best friends in the coaching profession, head coach Mike Price. Having the opportunity to mingle with those guys made it just the opposite of that Outback Bowl experience.

We fell behind 14-0 in the first quarter but then came back to make a game of it before losing, 33-27. Orton threw a 51-yard touchdown pass to Taylor Stubblefield with 1:53 remaining, and then we recovered an onside kick. We drove to the Washington State 22-yard line and had two wide-open receivers over the middle. If Orton could have gotten the pass off, I think we would have won, but a fifth-year senior blew a blocking assignment.

I've always tried to lighten up stuffy press conferences. This one was at the Sun Bowl in El Paso. Photo provided courtesy of the Journal-Courier (Lafayette, Indiana)

That game marked the beginning of the Kyle Orton era. We gave his right arm quite a workout that day as he completed 38 of 74 for 419 yards, two touchdowns, and four interceptions. Those 74 attempts were the most in NCAA bowl history and second-most for a Purdue quarterback. The 419 yards was the most for a Boilermaker freshman quarterback. Due to Orton's development over the second half of the 2001 season, we really felt like we had weathered the storm coming out of the Brees years. We had identified a new talent at quarterback who we felt was a very capable player. With Orton and great experience coming back on defense, we were feeling confident heading into the 2002 season.

We lost a real heartbreaker at Notre Dame, though, in the second game of 2002. The Fighting Irish beat us, 24-17, after they scored two touchdowns in 11 seconds early in the second quarter. They scooped up a fumble and returned it 54 yards, and then we fumbled the kickoff, and they ran it into the end zone. If that wasn't bad enough, Notre Dame scored the winning touchdown on a 33-yard interception return with just 5:09 remaining. Those turnovers spoiled a great performance by our defense, which held Notre Dame to 203 yards and 11 first downs.

Later that season, we lost three close games in a row—31-28 at Iowa, after Orton was knocked silly; 38-31 in overtime at Illinois; and 23-21 to Michigan. Then, two games later, we lost 10-6 to top-ranked Ohio State when the Buckeyes scored on a 37-yard, fourth-down touchdown pass with 1:36 on the clock. They went on to win the national championship, and champions have a way of making those plays.

The following week, I witnessed one of the most memorable plays I have ever seen during our 45-42 victory at Michigan State. Because of injuries, Brandon Kirsch started at quarterback in place of Orton. But with Purdue in possession at the MSU 40-yard line, Kirsch had the wind knocked out of him with less than four minutes remaining in the game. After standing on the sideline for more than three hours

During the game, I wore a NYPD cap, and Mike Price of Washington State wore a FDNY cap. Both departments were recognized at halftime. Photo provided courtesy of Purdue University Sports Information

in 30-degree weather, Orton entered the game after a couple warmup tosses. We had a play called to pick up a first down, but when Orton got up behind center, I could hear him checking into a different play. He was calling for a streak route to John Standeford. I kept yelling, "No, no, no!" And then Orton heaved it, and I was yelling, "Yes, yes, yes!" He threw a perfect pass down the left sideline, and Standeford caught it for a game-winning 40-yard touchdown.

For the second year in a row, we went to the Sun Bowl; but this time we broke a three-game bowl losing streak by beating Washington. We fell behind, 17-0, in the first quarter but came back to win, outscoring the Huskies 31-0 in the second and third quarters. Coming back to the Sun Bowl didn't concern me because of our experience playing in those two consecutive Alamo Bowl games. We had done it before. The irony of that second Sun Bowl game was that Washington beat us, 34-24, in the Rose Bowl, and we beat them by that same score in El Paso.

Chapter 14

A THIRD NEW YEAR'S DAY BOWL

We were a junior-dominated team in 2002, so I thought 2003 would be a year that we could seriously challenge for a Big Ten championship. We had to play both Michigan and Ohio State on the road, but it was going to be the senior season for the Stu Schweigert crew. All those recruits who came in with Stu were now seniors who had been starting for three and four years. We really thought it would be our best chance since 2000 to make a real run at the title. Although we didn't necessarily like our schedule, we liked our team.

It didn't take long for our team to face a reality check, as Bowling Green beat us at home in the season opener, 27-26. After that game, I scrimmaged the team on Sunday for the first—and only—time in my career as a head coach. Maybe that scrimmage got the players' attention—we reeled off six victories in a row before Michigan gave us yet another wakeup call in a 31-3 loss.

What followed was our toughest loss in my time at Purdue, a 16-13 overtime defeat at Ohio State. As a coach, you shouldn't do this, but I was convinced we were going to beat the Buckeyes in Columbus.

I just felt like the stars were aligned, and it was our year—that we were going to go into The Horseshoe and come out victorious. We weren't having a particularly great year, but I thought winning in Columbus would be a springboard to having a good season. That was a tough, tough loss because, if we had defeated the Buckeyes, we would have tied for the Big Ten championship.

The good news is that we were 9-3 during the regular season and made it back to a New Year's Day bowl—the Capital One Bowl in Orlando. We were matched up against a much, much, much faster Georgia team. Even though they were superior, we had a chance to win but ended up losing in overtime, 34-27—our second overtime loss to the Bulldogs in a Florida New Year's Day bowl in four years.

Unbelievably, Georgia jumped out to a 24-0 lead in the second quarter, so for us just to get back into that game took one of the most amazing performances I've seen in my coaching career. We tied the game on Ben Jones' 44-yard field goal in the final minute of regulation, but then the Bulldogs pulled it out in overtime.

Kyle Orton's performance that day was one of the most courageous I've ever seen. He suffered three injuries during that game—a dislocated thumb on the first series of the game; turf toe, which was so painful that we had to inject him at halftime to dull the pain so he could push off on his throws; and when we arrived back home, they discovered that he had a cracked rib. That was an unbelievably gutsy performance. To deal with all of the hurdles we had to overcome, pushing that game into overtime was really one of our better efforts of the year.

We had a good team with all those seniors, and it ranked among the most fun teams I'd coached. Despite losing to Bowling Green, despite losing to Ohio State in overtime, it was still a very exciting year. There was only one game in which we weren't competitive, and that was against Michigan in Ann Arbor—but we could have won the Bowling Green game, the Ohio State game, and the bowl game.

Another opportunity to point out to the officials the error of their ways—I lost this one, too.
Photo provided courtesy of Purdue University Sports Information

Following the 2003 season, after seven bowl games in seven seasons, we finally thought that our success was starting to pay dividends in recruiting. After that year, everything became a little bit easier—not significantly, but a little bit.

Despite the tremendous expectations before the 2003 season, I thought our chances to be successful were greater in 2004. We knew we had a quarterback who could take us a long way. We also knew that we had the weapons offensively at the skilled positions to complement him—a record-setting receiver in Taylor Stubblefield, among other quality receivers and a tight end who could catch the ball, a couple of good junior tailbacks, and a potential game-breaker in Dorien Bryant. Defensively, we graduated many of our players, but we returned a young, aggressive defense that we felt pretty good about.

Going into the season, I thought it might be our best year since 2000. When we started out with a 51-0 victory over Syracuse, I was pretty well convinced that '04 could be a good season. After beating Ball State and Illinois, winning handily at Notre Dame, 41-16, and then beating Penn State in Happy Valley, I thought, just maybe, it was going to be one of those fantastic years.

Unfortunately, the 2004 season forever will be remembered at Purdue as "The Year of the Fumble"—Orton's fumble in the 20-17 home loss to Wisconsin. I had a bad feeling during that game. When we had a 17-7 lead, one of our defensive backs dropped a sure interception, and the Badgers scored with less than six minutes to play. Trying to protect a 17-14 lead, we were facing a critical third-and-short situation, when we called a bootleg keeper for Orton. He had the first down—but then he was undercut, went head over heels, and spit out the ball. The Badgers recovered and returned it 40 yards for the winning touchdown. Looking back, though, I wouldn't change anything. Whenever you get into a tight situation, putting the ball in your best player's hands is the most prudent thing to do.

That game began an unbelievable string of four consecutive games that saw us lose by three points to Wisconsin (20-17), by two to

Michigan (16-14), by three to Northwestern (13-10), and by two to Iowa (23-21). That's 10 points that led to four straight losses. As a coach, I'd never had a string of close defeats like that before. Much was made of how great our young defense was playing. But the reality was, the defense had a difficult time closing out games. Our defense was not strong enough or talented enough to finish strong. We had the lead late in the fourth quarter in three of the four losses. The most interesting comments I heard from fans during that month was, "You know, Coach, I'd rather lose 35-7 than 16-14." My response was, "I would never choose to get blown out over having a chance to win."

We rallied to close out the regular season with a thrilling 24-17 victory over Ohio State and a surprisingly easy 63-24 victory over Indiana. During our preparations for the Hoosiers, Jim Chaney noticed on tape that, right before the half and sometimes at the end of games, Indiana didn't respond very well to the quick, no-huddle, two-minute passing game. We made the decision to come out and play the whole game that way—and, gee whiz, the scoreboard lit up, and it stayed lit up.

We took a 7-4 record to the Sun Bowl—our third trip to El Paso in four years—to play a very talented Arizona State team. That's one of the drawbacks with the Big Ten's agreement with the Sun Bowl. The toughest bowl draw, outside of our champion, is the team that goes to the Sun Bowl. The game matches the third-place team from the Pacific-10 Conference against the fifth- or sixth-place Big Ten team. The one thing we learned about the Sun Bowl is, you're always going to draw a good opponent. We drew Washington the year they were favored to go to the Rose Bowl, and two years earlier we played a very good Washington State team that had won 10 games. Those are tough matchups for any team. I was concerned about going back to the Sun Bowl for the third time, because I was afraid that our players might simply go through the motions.

It was a strange opening two quarters, as Arizona State led only 3-2 at halftime; but then both teams' offenses started getting in gear. We

Two of the most productive players we had at Purdue—Taylor Stubblefield (No. 21), the all-time leading pass catcher in NCAA history, and Kyle Orton (No. 18).
Photo provided courtesy of Purdue University Sports Information

alternated scoring drives in the second half before the Sun Devils prevailed, 27-23. We played a solid game against a very good team. But, once again, we had a lead with 43 seconds to go and couldn't hold on.

Unfortunately, we had some guys who, shall we say, "enjoyed themselves" too much in El Paso, which is why I was upset after the game and threatened to put our team in a monastery before future bowl games. But that was just emotion speaking—you're always walking a fine line at a bowl game, which is supposed to be a reward for the players.

It's a reward for what you did during 6 a.m. winter workouts on dark February mornings.

It's a reward for throwing your body around during spring scrimmages.

It's a reward for lifting weights in 98-degree weather during the summer.

So what do you do when you get to the bowl? How tightly do you rein them in? Our approach has always been to enjoy the experience—it's a life memory that the players take with them forever. We try to give the players a little bit of rope to run with but not so much that they hang themselves. Sometimes it works, and sometimes it doesn't.

Chapter 15

REALITY CHECK

Th">here were little telltale signs along the way, as early as our winter conditioning workouts, that our 2005 team had a different motivation. Actually, we thought the winter workouts before the season were as good, if not the best, that we'd had at Purdue. But then I tried something I had heard a coach talk about at a clinic. We were near the end of morning drills, and we had a particularly challenging day. Our guys had worked very hard that morning. However, after everyone had gathered around me, signaling the end of the workout, I said, "Hey guys, we're going into overtime. Back on the line—let's go. We're running more sprints."

We had some open rebellion at that point. About a half-dozen players didn't try to hide their dislike of having to run more. They had just put everything on the line, and we wanted more from them. I blew the whistle and said, "To hell with you guys. If you don't want to put out this effort to help you become a better football team, then the hell with you—just go on in."

Some of the older players decided they were going to run, but I told the coaches to get out—and we all left. The players did something on their own, but just the fact that this team—or at least the vocal players on the team—didn't want to buy into what it took to be a champion told me something. I didn't like it, and I filed it in the back of my mind. I didn't make a big deal out of it, but it was a minor red flag at the time. Because we had worked so hard during that workout, though, I didn't regard it as a major red flag.

Late that winter, the staff discussed forming a players' council to develop some team leadership. Jim Tressel had one at Ohio State, and Georgia coach Mark Richt told me that he had one and thought it was effective. After some discussion as a staff about which players should be on our players' council, we decided to include five seniors, four juniors, three sophomores, two freshmen, and a walk-on. We decided, "Maybe if we put them on this players' council, we could swing them over to our way of thinking. We could make them feel good about being part of this team." We ended up with probably five fence-sitting players—guys who could go either way—on the council, but we still thought, "If we could be inclusive and have them be a part of this, maybe it would be a really good thing for us."

We only had three meetings before I dissolved it. It basically became a bitch session. They had an opportunity to complain, and it became a "gimme" meeting—"gimme this, gimme that." The negative guys dominated the meetings. We did do some things they requested, but we didn't get any positive leadership in return. I happened to read a book later that spring about bringing out the best in people. To paraphrase the author, if you're ever going to put together a group within your company or organization to determine the policies and assume the leadership roles, you should pick the most positive people. I thought to myself, "Hey, idiot, you should have read this before you formed that players' council."

Spring ball that year was okay at best. We thought we'd be further ahead coming out of the spring but, overall, we weren't improving. If anything, we were flat. That was another hint that maybe this team wasn't going to be as good as everyone outside the program thought.

I suffered in silence in 2005. I've always said, "Losing is easy—not enjoyable, but easy."
Photo provided courtesy of the Journal-Courier (Lafayette, Indiana)

By NCAA rules, coaches aren't allowed to watch the players work out during the summer months. But that summer, I'd run into our strength coach, Jim Lathrop, and he'd say, "We had three guys skip a week's workout." We never had that happen in the past. This was the first time I ever heard Jim say, "These guys aren't working as hard as our previous teams worked." That bothered me for two reasons: (1) I didn't think it was a good indicator of where we were headed as a team; and (2) Jim is a very hard worker, and he was opening up the weight room at five or six o'clock in the morning to accommodate guys. He was going out of his way to make the facility available, and some guys weren't taking advantage of that. We also had some players skip our team barbecue, which was a first. That again told me that some of our guys had their own agendas.

During my vacation in July, I received a telephone call informing me that two of our offensive linemen had gotten into a fight during one of the volunteer summer workouts. Uche Nwaneri, a starter, was arrested; and Ryan Noblet, a reserve, suffered a broken jaw. According to the information I received, Nwaneri was trying to become a vocal leader. One guy wasn't working as hard as the rest of the group, and another guy challenged him on it. That led to a verbal confrontation, which led to a pushing match and, finally, a swing. When I arrived back on campus three days later, I found out that the university was going to suspend Nwaneri for the fall semester, so I conducted my own investigation. Knowing the personalities and knowing the sources, I concluded that the guy who was being charged was no more in the wrong than the guy who had been hit—as a matter of fact, the guy who was hit was just as guilty, if not more so, and I interviewed more people who witnessed the altercation than the university officials did.

The next thing I knew, after camp started, we had a starter who was suspended for the fall semester. That certainly upset him, and it upset a lot of our players, who didn't think his situation was handled justly. Nwaneri appealed the university's suspension, but we made the decision not to practice him with the first team just in case his suspension was upheld. That kept the topic alive. About a week before our first game, we finally got a ruling that Nwaneri was ineligible to play in 2005. I found it interesting that the other player involved in the scuffle transferred to the University of Arkansas, where he washed out of their football program after one semester. He eventually transferred to the University of Indianapolis to be closer to his mother, but the media picked up on none of this.

During two-a-days, I kicked our starting safety, junior Bernard Pollard, out of practice and suspended him for a few days. I was hoping to get the same results from the year before, when I did the same thing with linebacker Bobby Iwuchukwu. When Bobby came back, he was a much better guy with a better attitude. He got the message. Some guys get it, and some guys don't get it. Apparently, Pollard didn't get it, because, when he came back, he was reserved, which was totally the opposite from his usual outgoing personality. We had many discussions, and he was very good in our one-on-one talks. But I didn't realize that, apparently from the day I kicked him out of practice, his resentment towards the program—and towards me specifically—continued to grow.

Anyone who has been around Bernard knows that he is a volatile guy with a short fuse. The problem was his temper, and I could see him hurting the team at some point in the season. Controlled volatility in the sport of football can be good, but I suggested that perhaps he should spend some time with people who could help him control his anger issues. Initially, he agreed, and I think he had one meeting with a professional, but that was it. Throughout the fall, I tried to—I don't want to say, "reconcile"—but be civil toward him. If he played well, I would congratulate him after a game. I would see him in the hall and ask him how he was doing. I'd ask him how school was going. Each time, he was very short with me. Little did we know that he had already made his decision—one he never shared with me—to declare early for the

Practices in 2005 were much different than this 1997 session.
Photo provided courtesy of Purdue University Sports Information

NFL draft. When we finished the season, he returned to his home in Fort Wayne and never came back to campus to finish his classes that semester. He took four 'Fs' as a result. What a shame.

From the opening game, Ray Edwards, our starting junior defensive end, obviously had an individual agenda as well. A Purdue grad wrote me to wish us the best of luck, and he commented that he hoped our players were more interested in being a team than a group of individuals. He had noticed at our season opener that the team had run onto the field, but that Edwards had walked out, trailing 50 yards behind the last player.

I've always tried to be the last guy out of our locker room, and I noticed that there were about a half-dozen players who had developed an "I" contest during the 2005 season—to see who could be the last guy out of the locker room. If you're the last player out, everybody sees you. One time, I actually found a guy hiding in the restroom. I had to go back and get him out of a stall. Things like that indicated that, collectively, we were an immature team.

During a Sunday staff meeting following the fourth or fifth game, our coaches asked me if I'd seen the "prayer pods." I had never heard of the term, and I didn't know what that was. Apparently, when our team came out onto the field, a group of our players would go to the end zone, kneel down, and pray. The coaches noted that, while a group of players was clustered in the corner of the end zone in one of these "prayer pods," one guy would be taking a knee all by himself in the middle of the end zone. Again, that was Ray Edwards. I told his position coach to talk to him, and I even spoke to our team chaplain. I asked him if I was being insensitive by saying we should be a team. I wanted direction from a man of the cloth. He talked to the players, quoting scripture, which I put in my book of notes:

"And when you pray, do not be like the hypocrites, for they love to pray standing in the synagogues and on the street corners to be seen by men. I tell you the truth, they have received their reward in full. But when you pray, go into your room, close the door, and pray to your

Father, who is unseen. Then your Father, who sees what is done in secret, will reward you."

Each spring, I meet with every player and ask him how he thinks we'll do that next season. I make them predict our record. I think this is important because I always want a team that believes they will be successful. Our first year, we had some guys who thought we'd have a losing record, but since then we've never had anybody predict that we wouldn't have a winning season—not one player.

In the spring of 2005, I met with the 84 players on our roster. Here's how they voted:

12 - 0	17
11 - 1	18
10 - 2	30
9 - 3	10
8 - 4	8
7 - 5	1

My thought was, "I'll take 10-2 right now without playing a single game." My guess was, "We'll be an 8-4 team." I always put my prediction in an envelope, seal it, and open it at the end of the season. I believed that because (1) we were going with an unproven quarterback; and (2) in spite of what others thought, we knew our defense was suspect, with very little depth in the secondary. Before the 2005 season, I thought I did a very poor job of managing the expectations, which were running wild. We had some reasons to be optimistic, but the atmosphere was almost euphoric in nature. That's never good.

Selling tickets is one of a Purdue coach's jobs. At some schools, coaches don't have to worry about selling tickets, but I'm more likely to put my foot in my mouth due to my obligation to sell tickets. I don't like that, but that's a reality of life. The last thing the Purdue athletic director or president wants is a football coach who is going to stand up and rain on everybody's parade. When Lou Holtz was at Notre Dame, he was perhaps the master of badmouthing his own team and building up opponents. But Lou didn't have to sell any tickets. If you took that approach at Purdue, why would anybody come watch your team? Those expectations carried their own momentum on a national level, but maybe I could have lessened their impact locally.

I made a comment in Chicago, at the Big Ten Kickoff, that we'd go as far as the quarterback position goes. I figured that we better be a heck of a lot better defensively than we were in 2004 because we weren't going to be nearly as potent offensively. Everybody was back on defense but, really, how good was that defense? As I said, you don't want to rain on anybody's parade, so you don't point those things out. The coaches may know in the staff room, but you don't go public with your evaluation of exactly where you are. I should have made statements such as, "We really still are inexperienced on defense," and, "We don't have a lot of depth on defense." I should have talked about how we needed to take a wait-and-see approach regarding exactly how good we were, particularly on the defensive side of the ball.

We made a concerted effort to try to adjust the offense to the talents of the quarterback personnel. Knowing that Brandon Kirsch wasn't as good a passer as the guy who just walked out the door, we knew we were going to have to do some things offensively to make up some ground. We put in some option because Kirsch had been a very effective scrambler the two seasons he had gotten some playing time. But we found out that Brandon really wasn't capable of handling all of the intricacies of running the option. The reality was, he was better running a broken play than he was with a designed play. And as the season unfolded, we had guys open in the passing game, but we couldn't get them the ball.

On the outside, we were presenting a rosy picture, but the staff knew we had some real limitations. Maybe what I said publicly wouldn't have made any difference—I probably couldn't have slowed down the hype. The further away from Purdue you got, the better we were as a team. People from Dallas, Seattle, or Boston, who were evaluating the Big Ten, were picking us to win it or finish as the runner-up. The *Orlando Sentinel* even picked us No. 1 in its preseason Top-25 rankings.

That we didn't have Michigan or Ohio State on our schedule was not as significant to our coaching staff as it became to everyone else in the world—the fans, our local media, the national media, the players, the players' families, and the students at Purdue. Everybody kept harping on the fact that we didn't have the Buckeyes or the Wolverines on our schedule. I'm sure that fanned the flame of expectations. I kept saying, "We need to focus on who *is* on our schedule, rather than who is *not* on our schedule." The onslaught against that way of thinking, though, was overwhelming. Young people tend to get ahead of themselves, and maybe that's why we didn't work as hard during the summer. They knew Michigan and Ohio State weren't on the schedule—and they were being reminded of that all the time.

We had another problem in that season. I'd often tell our coaches not to be blinded by our recruited talent. Some of those guys had their own aforementioned agendas, which happened to be self-promotion. The question is: as a coach, why didn't I correct that? In the staff room, we often discussed solutions, but we really didn't have any alternatives. Had we gone out and recruited several junior-college players over the previous couple of years, we'd have been better prepared to make those adjustments. But we hadn't. More than once, I told the staff, "We can make a change at that position today—right now. You guys tell me whom we should put in. C'mon, give me a name—who should we

Our 2005 team presented new challenges. Photo provided courtesy of Purdue University Sports Information

use?" In a sense, we were being held hostage. We didn't have enough options, and my question to the staff was met by dead silence.

To the media, that should have become very obvious. They did notice it, but I'm surprised it wasn't a bigger story. In the middle of the season, we moved Brandon Whittington, and then Ray Williams, from receiver to defensive back. Those were unprecedented moves. I'm kind of surprised the media didn't say, "These guys are in trouble, and they know it. This is a desperation move." When the season started, we didn't realize how fragile the team was defensively. Perhaps I give the media too much credit at times. Sometimes I do think one of the pluses of dealing with the media is that they ask some questions that get you thinking as a coach. I think the media are pretty damn good really, but I thought they missed how desperate and tenuous our defensive situation had become.

The best way to describe the beginning of the 2005 season, unlike at any other time since we've been at Purdue, is that we were walking a tightrope without a safety net. We had to have many things go exactly right for us just to come close to meeting the expectations. One thing I've observed over the years is that, on most teams, there are good kids and then there are the fence-sitters. When things go well, the fence-sitters walk the line. If things go bad, they fall off the fence on the opposite side. That happened to us as our 2005 season progressed. As we started to lose some games, it got uglier. If we, as coaches, did one thing well in 2005, it was that we stayed positive— maybe more than normal under what were very trying circumstances.

The third game of the season, when we lost in overtime at Minnesota, 42-35, was an indication that we were in trouble defensively. Yet, unquestionably, the turning point of the season was the following week, when we lost at home to Notre Dame, 49-28. Our weaknesses were exposed in that game. I knew Notre Dame was a good team—I had some friends on Ty Willingham's staff, and they all were convinced that would have been their best team. As we were getting ready to play Notre Dame in 2005, I thought it was going to be a real

Walking a tightrope without a net—the 2005 season.
Photo provided courtesy of Purdue University Sports Information.

test. Publicly, I wasn't saying it, but as I compared that team to our team, I knew their offense was superior to our defense—not *better* than our defense, *superior* to our defense. I knew we were in trouble. I just didn't want to admit to the world how much trouble.

One of the most challenging things about coaching is that today's young people have become more reluctant to step up and speak out, to correct a teammate. Everything today seems to be about "fitting in." I had a real good meeting with our seniors after we lost our sixth game, after we were out of bowl contention. During that meeting, I pointed out to the seniors how they weren't correcting teammates when they were doing the wrong things; that they were worried more about their buddies and fitting in with the crowd, being accepted socially. All that was falling on the coaches, and, after a while, as a coach you get tired of continuously dropping the hammer. Coaches need help from their players—from their leaders—and we just weren't getting it.

After that talk, some guys did step up and say some things to other players. We won our last three games, for a number of reasons—some seniors stepped up; we made some personnel moves that began to pay off; and our last three opponents weren't as good as some of our earlier opponents. If I could have done anything different during the 2005 season, it would have been to have that meeting with the seniors after the third or fourth loss. After the sixth loss, it was too late. At the beginning of every season, I always tell the players that the team will be as good as its senior class. I do this to motivate the seniors—the ones in the best position to lead—and to challenge them. Yet, in 2005, although we had a good senior class, those players simply weren't natural leaders. They were, however, good people.

Chapter 16

TERRIFIC TRIO—
DICKEN, BREES,
ORTON

Having been an assistant coach at Purdue from 1983 to 1986, I became very familiar with its reputation as "The Cradle of Quarterbacks." Former Boilermaker quarterbacks such as Len Dawson, Bob Griese, Mike Phipps, Mark Herrmann, and Jim Everett are just a few of the members of that elite group. Griese, Phipps, Herrmann, and Everett were All-Americans. Dawson, with Kansas City, and Griese, with Miami, both quarterbacked teams to Super Bowl victories.

During our relatively short stay at Purdue, we've been fortunate to coach three quarterbacks who are now considered to be part of The Cradle of Quarterbacks—Billy Dicken, Drew Brees (who also was an All-American), and Kyle Orton.

The question now is, will Curtis Painter become the next member of the club? I think he has that kind of potential. I hope I'm not overrating this kid, but the more I'm around him, the more I'm beginning to see the same qualities, the same attributes, the same skills that these other quarterbacks possessed. Here's hoping it comes to fruition.

Billy Dicken (1994 to 1997)

Our first year at Purdue, we had a guy who was a real Mississippi River boat gambler. Billy Dicken was a player who would take a chance—he would pull the ball down and run, or he would throw the ball into coverage without thinking twice about it. He was a risk taker and an excellent competitor.

Before we arrived at Purdue, Dicken had suffered two injuries to his right (throwing) shoulder—first he dislocated it, and then he suffered a torn rotator cuff. Billy wasn't looking so good when we were installing our spread offense that first spring. In fact, after the spring game, we decided that John Reeves was our starting quarterback. But then we went through our two-a-days in August, and Dicken started running the offense better than Reeves, so we ended up going with Dicken.

Billy wasn't the most consistent passer. Every game, he would end up one-bouncing a bubble-screen pass. We used to laugh about it as a staff. Every week in the staff room, we'd wonder at what point of the game he was going to bounce-pass to somebody, whether it was a curl route, a hook route, or a swing route. Sometime during the game, he was going to one-hop it to somebody. We'd become frustrated with him because he wasn't the most accurate passer, but every game he made some very impressive throws and some big plays.

Dicken was an unpredictable quarterback for the opponents and, sometimes, for our own coaching staff. That made him an exciting guy. He had a good football mind, and that helped him. I really liked Billy Dicken because he was a gamer. He was better on Saturday than he was during the week, and I haven't seen many guys like that during my coaching career.

I've often been asked, especially when Drew Brees was our starter, "Is it the system or is it the quarterback?" In Dicken's case, our system unquestionably revitalized, kick-started, and recharged his career. He was on a slow train headed nowhere, and this offense gave him a new life. Brees executed the offense better than anyone else; and Orton did a great job of fitting into the system; but Dicken maximized his opportunity better than anyone. Billy was the greatest benefactor of our element of surprise. Back then, the defensive coordinators weren't as well prepared to defend our offense as they've eventually become.

Dicken was in the system for only one year. To come off the depths of the bench at training camp to being voted first-team All-Big Ten by the conference coaches—how does it get any better than that? It doesn't.

The only problem I had with Billy, who was 21 or 22 when he was a senior, was standing next to him during our Sunday workout. That whiskey breath he had could knock you over. That's the way he lived his life. He lived hard, and he played hard. He reminded me of ol' Bobby Layne, the former great quarterback for the Detroit Lions—who they used to say never lost a game; time just ran out on him.

Dicken was a throwback-type guy. He loved the game, and he loved celebrating after the game.

Drew Brees (1997 to 2000)

The recruitment of Drew Brees was an interesting situation. All kinds of stories arose about who did and didn't recruit him—especially that nobody in Texas recruited him. That wasn't true. The two big schools, Texas and Texas A&M, didn't recruit him, but other schools in Texas did try to sign him—they just weren't upper-echelon schools. It came down to Kentucky or Purdue, two programs that were running similar offenses, so Drew knew that both programs were going to feature the pass as their primary mode of transportation.

Drew's parents are both attorneys, so perhaps the consensus around the house was that Purdue was a better choice academically; but I actually think he liked the Kentucky campus better than the Purdue campus. The weather was miserable our first winter at

Purdue, including the weekend of Drew's official visit. It was so cold that December when those kids came up from Texas that we left the cars running so we could drive them from one building to the next—so cold that we didn't want them to walk the one block from the football building to our training table at Cary Quad. We had three consecutive weekends with that kind of weather, but we got lucky; the weather wasn't an issue with some of those guys, including Drew Brees.

Coming out of high school, Drew's arms looked like pencils. He looked like anything but a Big Ten football player. Tim Lappano, one of our assistants, had been recruiting for us in Texas, and he went down there for a playoff game. After watching Drew practice, he called and said that we should offer this kid. It was late November or early December of his senior year, and we hadn't offered him yet, but Lappano raved about the way he put the ball right on the numbers. So I said, "Let's go on him." When Drew picked Purdue, we knew we had a good quarterback; but as you have read, we didn't know how excellent he'd become.

We liked what we saw from Drew from day one in training camp. Everyone agreed, "Wow, this guy can really throw the ball."

Though we thought we had a good player, we still didn't think we had a star. In fact, that was the year we recruited and signed David Edgerton. We were so convinced that Drew was going to be a star that we recruited a junior-college quarterback to compete with him for the job.

"Coach Tiller is like an amateur psychologist. A saying that he always used was, 'Do what you're supposed to do, when you're supposed to do it, the way it's supposed to be done, and do it that way every time.' You hear that enough times, you live your life like that. That's absolutely engrained in me."

Drew Brees

Drew's first start for Purdue, as a sophomore in 1998, was our season opener at the Los Angeles Coliseum against Southern Cal in the Pigskin Classic. That was the game he scrambled to his right and threw a strike for a touchdown pass. The moment we scored on that play, I said into my headset, "We've got ourselves a quarterback, boys."

Brees truly had a Cinderella year as a sophomore. At the start of that season, I'm not sure anyone at Purdue knew exactly how big of an impact he would have on the program. That year we discovered how much he really enjoyed the two-minute game. He liked practicing the two-minute drill, and he loved it during the game, which is indicative of an outstanding competitor. He may have been the best practice player we've ever had at Purdue—in fact, he may be the best practice player I've ever been around, period.

He threw a bazillion touchdown passes (actually, *only* six) that year against Minnesota and then came back the next week at Wisconsin and threw an NCAA-record 83 passes. He completed 55, which tied another NCAA record. He was intercepted four times, including twice in the end zone. While that would crush most guys, Drew had the ability to let go of a mistake or a bad game immediately and move on, which is very rare, and only the great ones can pull it off.

Our great comeback in the Alamo Bowl that season against fourth-ranked Kansas State defined our year. When Drew drove us down the field in the final seconds for the winning touchdown, that's when he really crashed the national scene. His decision-making was flawless. The final throw for the touchdown, when he put it over the defender and right over the shoulder of Isaac Jones, was perfect. That stamped him as a national player.

The media requests for Drew started strong and then skyrocketed as his junior year progressed. To give you an idea of what Drew Brees meant to us, in 1997, I thought we were snubbed by the Outback Bowl. We had finished ahead of Wisconsin in the final Big Ten standings; and we had defeated the Badgers on the field. Yet the Outback Bowl bypassed us and picked the Badgers for their game. Now, in Drew's junior season in 1999, we were a 7-4 team, 4-4 in the league and tied for sixth; and yet, the Outback Bowl took us. They did that because they wanted Drew Brees.

Clowning around with Drew Brees (at the request of the media, I might add).
Photo provided courtesy of the Journal-Courier (Lafayette, Indiana)

The one thing I regretted that year was not going to New York for the Heisman Trophy award ceremony. I knew Drew wasn't going to win the Heisman—he ended up finishing fourth—so I didn't go. I didn't think it was that significant. After watching it on television, I knew that I should have been there. Even though I didn't know if he would be invited back the next year, I decided right then that, if he was a Heisman finalist again, I was going to New York.

By the time Drew's senior season rolled around, he was the calendar boy. He excelled at handling pressure, on the field and off. His management of the media attention was exceptional. The media liked him because he was a very mature and patient guy. His senior year was the first time ever that we assigned security to a player. There was a fan-feeding frenzy for him after games. Home games were unbearable—the guy couldn't get out of the locker room, and it got to the point where it became a little dangerous. During his junior year, we had some young fans fall down the stairs outside our locker room while trying to get to him after a game.

Finally, during his senior year, Drew parked his car by Lambert Fieldhouse, and, after he dealt with the media, he would use the tunnels from the Intercollegiate Athletic Facility, which houses our locker boom, to Mackey Arena and then to Lambert. We would whisk him underground two buildings away, so he could get to his car and drive off. He was a guy who truly endeared himself to the fans, his teammates, and the media. That can be said of very few athletes, especially at Drew's age. He was beyond his years.

The three defining Drew Brees moments were the touchdown pass against Southern Cal, the final drive in the Alamo Bowl; and the pass to Seth Morales to beat Ohio State. The most thrilling moment of his entire career, for me, was standing on that field after we beat Indiana his senior season as Drew walked around with a rose clinched between his teeth, knowing that we were going to the Rose Bowl.

Drew Brees had the biggest impact of any player I've been around as a coach. He helped to elevate Purdue from a good team to a national program.

Kyle Orton (2001 to 2004)

After Drew Brees' lights-out sophomore year, we had a difficult time recruiting a quarterback. As he became a senior, though, we suddenly had more national quarterbacks interested in us, and we were able to sign Kyle Orton.

The more we watched Orton in practice during his freshman year, the more impressed we were with him. As a true freshman, he became our No. 2 quarterback, behind Brandon Hance. With two games remaining in our regular season, we made the change to Orton. He was a strong-armed guy, and he demonstrated that right from the get-go. Of his three starts as a freshman, his most impressive performance came during a 33-27 loss to Washington State in the Sun Bowl. He got off to a horrendous start—his first pass, an interception, was returned 45 yards for a touchdown. But he threw 74 passes that day, which set an all-time bowl record. Even though he was intercepted four times, he was very impressive—completing 38 passes for 419 yards and two touchdowns.

As a sophomore, Orton suffered a concussion in our game at Iowa. The coaching staff didn't know he had a problem until one of the other players came off the field and said, "Coach, he just called a play that we don't even have." He was clearly out on his feet, so we replaced him with Brandon Kirsch. Orton came back after that Iowa game, but he struggled. He never wanted you to know when he was hurt, so I don't know how long that concussion lingered. He really had a lot of pride in being tough, but we didn't know that about him during his sophomore year. Orton struggled to the point that we eventually made Kirsch the starter. Kyle wasn't happy about that, but he said all the right things. I knew what he was feeling and what he was saying were two different things, but that demonstrated to me that he was really a team guy and a mature guy. Orton's winning touchdown pass, coming off the bench at Michigan State, was one of the most impressive throws I've ever seen—and he was just a sophomore.

Kyle was poised to have a very big year as a junior, but that was the season we had all those outstanding starters returning on defense. Most of them were three- or four-year starters. As a result, the staff decided that we should rein in the offense a little bit, to eliminate some of the high-risk throws. We decided that we were good enough on defense to win most games if we didn't put them in bad situations. Orton, a strong-armed guy who was coming into his own, could have been a jerk, but he went along with that philosophy. He executed the game plans and never complained. Kyle's performance in the Capital

Coming off the field with Kyle Orton after his big game at Notre Dame in 2004.
Photo provided courtesy of the Journal-Courier (Lafayette, Indiana)

One Bowl that year—playing with a dislocated thumb, a sprained big toe, and a cracked rib—was one of the gutsiest I've ever seen.

Orton's senior year was marred by *the fumble* during our loss to Wisconsin, which is a shame; because on that play anybody would have had difficulty hanging on to the ball. He was hit, and he did a cartwheel, with his feet going above his head. He could have broken his neck when he came down, but he put out his hand to break his fall and the ball came loose. But that play is remembered as *the fumble* and the turning point of the season, which I don't think is fair. We all contributed to that loss, beginning with the defense.

The next week, he suffered a hip pointer in the first series against Michigan. Then, the following week against Northwestern, he tore a muscle on the opposite side. He couldn't play against Iowa, and he didn't start the Ohio State game. However, in that close contest against the Buckeyes, we got to our two-minute game at the end, and we thought a partially injured Kyle Orton could execute it better than a healthy Brandon Kirsch. We put Kyle in the game, and he took us right down the field for the winning touchdown. He completed each of his six passes with flawless execution—in spite of limited practice that week.

Orton doesn't possess the same status at Purdue as Brees, but if the timing of their careers would have been reversed, he probably could have done exactly what Brees did. Orton's arm was stronger than Drew's, but Brees had the edge in accuracy. However, during Orton's senior year, though, it was amazing how many times he put the ball on the body. Maybe under different circumstances—without the injuries and without playing in a close-to-the-vest offense as a junior—his numbers could have been just as impressive as Drew's. As a matter of fact, Drew called that season after our Notre Dame victory and said, "Tell Kyle I hope he breaks every Purdue passing record." He was on track, before the injuries, to do exactly that—break every Purdue passing record.

Drew played a big role in the recruitment of Kyle and really liked him.

I became closer to Kyle because he had a couple of quarterback coaches; and Brees had only one, Greg Olson, with whom he became very close friends. I got along very well with Drew, but I was closer to Kyle, and we had a unique relationship. One thing I appreciated most about Kyle Orton was that he wasn't a selfish guy.

Drew and Kyle were much alike—neither one was obsessed or infatuated with himself.

Chapter 17

BASKETBALL ON GRASS

(AKA SISSY BALL)

During our stay at Purdue, the media has used a couple of nicknames to describe the one-back spread offense—"Basketball on Grass" and "Sissy Ball." I really shouldn't blame the media, as I provided them with those terms to describe our style of play.

Looking back, though, two things about the term "Basketball on Grass" did bother me:

First, saying that we were playing basketball on grass didn't dignify the Purdue basketball program, which was among the nation's best when we arrived. I didn't want to suggest that we were trying to take away from everything the basketball program had accomplished. Nor did I want anybody to misinterpret the term as a reference to Coach Gene Keady and all the great things he had achieved with his program. I certainly didn't mean to compare our program to his, because it didn't.

Secondly, I didn't like the phrase because it implied that you were avoiding physical confrontation in the sport of football, which allegedly is a manly sport.

The nickname "Sissy Ball" is my term. I invented it while speaking to Joe Paterno when we played Penn State during our first season at Purdue. I had known Coach Paterno for several years and had seen him at meetings, but this was the first time I talked with him on the field.

We were having a good year, and, before that first game against the Nittany Lions, Coach Paterno was very complimentary. He said, "C'mon Joe, you guys aren't going to spread us all out and throw the ball all over the place today, are you?" And it hit me. Here's Penn State—Linebacker U. They're going to knock you down and rub your face in it. So I said, "Yeah, Coach, that's all we know how to do. We just play Sissy Ball."

He laughed, and I've used that term ever since.

Actually, Basketball on Grass doesn't bother me as much as Sissy Ball. If I had to take back one of the two, I'd take back Sissy Ball. With Sissy Ball, you can offend the players in your system, although that's not the point. The point is that the spread offense is finesse football.

My first exposure to the spread offense came from Jack Elway, John's father.

John's coach at Granada Hills High School in California was running the spread, and Jack liked what he saw. Jack, who had run parts of the spread when he was the head coach at Cal State-Northridge, had become the head coach at San Jose State. I went to visit him, and that was the first time in my life I ever saw an empty backfield.

I really respected Jack Elway's football mind. He and I coached together at Washington State in the '70s and ran the split-back veer, triple-option style of offense. We hardly ever threw the ball. The spread offense intrigued me, so I asked him, "What's the perfect offense?"

"I think the perfect offense—if you could ever put it together—would be the one-back, spread-passing game with some form of the option," he told me.

That was about 25 years ago, and here we are running it today.

The problem is, both the spread and the option are very time-consuming, so coaches—including me—never thought you could devote enough time to the one-back spread and enough time to the option to make both effective. That's changing. Now that we've spent a year running the spread-option, I kick myself in the butt for not going to it earlier. After watching it, the option is much easier to teach out of the shotgun than it was out of the old split-back veer. Out of the shotgun, the quarterback is making his decisions three and four yards behind the line of scrimmage instead of at the line of scrimmage. That's like night and day.

I had forgotten all about that conversation with Jack Elway until I went to Wyoming as an assistant. We came in after Dennis Erickson had been the head coach, and they had run the spread offense for one year before he left for Washington State. Suddenly, I was being asked to coach the spread after having only heard about it while having a beer and talking with Jack Elway several years earlier. Erickson's staff left a playbook behind—which I still have. It's not even an inch thick. But the offense was so popular with the fans that, when Paul Roach took over the program, there was no doubt that Wyoming was going to continue to run the spread. We really had no choice. They had been running the wishbone at Wyoming for years, which was very boring compared to "Air Erickson."

When I look back, what we were doing was so elementary it was almost a joke. The offense was very simple. We only had a couple dozen plays, and we just kept running them over and over. Paul Roach had retained Larry Korpitz and Mark Tommerdahl from Erickson's staff. That proved to be a godsend. Larry was a student of the game; he knew that offense; and he was a good point of reference for us—as was Mark. It was a gutsy move, because most of us on that staff had never coached the spread offense. We soon learned that there were some real holes in the pass protection. We had to improve that part of the offense, so we began to make some changes. We started out by learning on the run, but I was excited about getting involved with the offense because I saw the potential.

In the beginning, some of the ways we were defended were unbelievable. As we used to say, it was like taking candy from a baby.

I credit Larry Korpitz, who was the quarterback coach, for the biggest change that occurred at Wyoming. We dabbled in it, but we didn't know what we were doing with the no-back formations. We ran it, but we really weren't quite sure why we ran it. Yet, Larry just fell in love with that formation, and he was the guy who added more to the passing game than we had been using in that formation. The offense was beginning to evolve.

Paul Roach had coached in the NFL under John Ralston and Red Miller at Denver, and then under John Madden at Oakland. He loved Madden's goal-line offense, so we ran the spread offense all over the field except at the goal line—where we ran Coach Madden's offense, and it was good to us. After two years, I went to Washington State with Mike Price, and he liked what we were doing, so he put in that same goal-line offense.

When I went to Washington State, I really believed that this was the offense of the future. Mike sent me down to visit Dennis Erickson, who then was the head coach at Miami. When I became the head coach at Wyoming, there was no doubt we were going to run this stuff. Larry Korpitz had left Wyoming to be the head coach at Chico State and then had gone to New Mexico as an assistant. I thought it was critical to get him on the staff.

When we showed up at Purdue, some people suggested—before we had ever played a game—that we couldn't run this offense in the Big Ten Conference and in the cold, rain, and snow of the Midwest. But the only thing that really bothers the offense is wind—not rain, snow, temperature, or field conditions. I knew we dealt with much more wind in Wyoming than we would in the Midwest. Jim Wacker had run some spread offense when he was the head coach at Minnesota, but it was different from what we were running. We were putting more pres-

> "We were all just kind of waiting for someone to take the spread offense to the Big Ten. I thought it would take the conference by surprise, and I thought it would work. I didn't know it was going to be as great as it was. Joe did an awesome job and turned that Purdue program around very quickly."
>
> Mike Price

sure on the defenses, running more no-back stuff. Glen Mason changed the offense when he became the head coach at Minnesota the same year we came to Purdue, so we were the only team in the Big Ten that was running the spread. Today, every Big Ten team runs some form of the one-back spread.

Our first couple of years in the Big Ten were like starting all over again at Wyoming. It was unbelievable how we were being defended—you just knew some of their defensive concepts didn't have a chance. As a staff, we would snicker at some of the defenses we saw. But there isn't any snickering taking place anymore, because defenses are smacking us around. They've all wised up!

We had learned at Wyoming—long before we came to Purdue—that the system was very good, but it was much more effective when you had a talented quarterback. We won a couple of championships there, and it seemed like, when we had a good year, it was because we had a good, experienced quarter-back. Part of it is the system, but a bigger part of it is the talent at that position. The same can be said at Purdue. We know the offense is designed to put tremendous pressure on any defense that's out there, but you need the right guy pulling the trigger.

> "Some coaches were skeptical, but I never had any doubts that the spread offense would work in the Big Ten. In fact, it probably worked better there because Joe caught many of them off guard. Back then the Big Ten had a lot of big, strong guys, and he could spread them out and make those guys defend the whole field. The offense worked better there because they weren't prepared for it."
>
> Sonny Lubick

Having said that, it was infinitely easier when we first came to Purdue. Defenses in the Big Ten were not used to our style of offense. As I often describe the results, we were forcing many people to play left-handed (considering that we live in a right-handed world).

While we had an advantage early, Big Ten coaches are very competitive, and they began to pool their thoughts, ideas, and experiences on how best to defend the spread. As we were having one-back clinics on the evolution of the offense, others were having defensive clinics on how to stop it. Around 1999, coaches became very serious, and we became the focal point of many of our opponents. We found that, after we played an opponent in 1999 and 2000, the following team had all the information from the opponent we'd just played. Coaches were literally conspiring against us, particularly during the off-season. There was more communication than normal in an attempt to slow down this offense. Now, we are faced with the constant challenge of trying to stay a page ahead.

We could do that in 1997 and 1998 because we could anticipate the evolution of those adjustments. We could tell what they were going to go to next; until they finally exhausted all those options, and the chess match began in earnest around 2000—although I think the most dramatic changes have occurred during the past three years. People do a much better job today. They've recruited to defend the offense, and they've substituted personnel to defend the offense. Our first couple of years at Purdue, when we broke the huddle and lined up, there were some unbelievable mismatches. You might have a run-stopper covering a scat back in the passing game.

The rules have also changed. We developed a hurry-up offense, where we could change the formations after the team broke the huddle. The team would break the huddle, start to the line of scrimmage, and then two guys would come off the field; and two others would run out and line up in their place. Defensive coaches didn't like that, particularly the head coaches in the Big Ten, who were defensive in nature. They cried—and that's an acceptable word to use—and

After an early score in the 2000 Outback Bowl. We should have saved one for the overtime!
Photo provided courtesy of Purdue University Sports Information

pouted like children because they felt as if some of the things this offense utilized were giving it a distinct advantage over the defenses.

So the NCAA changed the rules to placate the pouters. It eliminated some of our options, like our substitutions from the sideline immediately to the formation. The new rule requires that a player has to run inside the yard-line numbers before he can come back out to line up. This allowed the defenses to settle down, identify what your formation was, and identify your personnel. They could make their substitutions after the huddle was broken, but the offense couldn't. Obviously, there have been some rule changes that directly help defend this offense.

In the last three years, defenses have developed pressure packages, most of which have filtered down from the pro level. In response, we've expanded the offense to include the option game. In more than one press conference, I've stood in front of the media and talked about how defending the option truly becomes assignment-oriented defense. When you don't take care of your assignment, big plays occur against you. During the 2005 season, we observed that defenses were making sure they had the option covered. As a result, we were seeing fewer defensive looks than we saw three years ago.

"What Joe Tiller has been able to do at Purdue and Wyoming has been among the top coaching performances in all of football. Over the many years we have known each other, it has become obvious to all that Joe is an outstanding coach with a great football mind."

Bill Polian

So the chess match continues.

Usually football is cyclical, but this offense is one that can withstand the test of time. I don't think college football—or high school football—will go back to a more conservative approach offensively, because we have to maintain a style of play that appeals to young people. When we are no longer attractive to young people, our numbers will begin to dwindle, and the total game itself will suffer. So, in this ATM society of fast-food and instant gratification, we must maintain a style of play that fascinates our youth. Spreading it out and throwing it around is a heck of a lot more appealing than bunching it up and pounding out the yards.

Somebody once asked me why we went to the spread offense, and, tongue in cheek, I said that it was at my wife's request. Arnette was not a big football fan before we got married. She had to learn the game over a long, long period. When we were running the Winged-T, she couldn't see the football. However, when we went to the spread and threw it out there, everybody could see the ball, and fans loved the offense.

Is the spread and option football perhaps the epitome of modern offense? I would suggest that it is. What's going to be the key in stopping it in the future? As anything, the more you see it, the more familiar it becomes, the more you can respond and react to it, and the less you are fooled.

One of two things can happen—either you adjust defensively to address the way you're being attacked, or you legislate against it. From an offensive point of view, I am wholly in favor of changing only one rule in college football that would parallel the NFL. I think too much of what we do is geared to what they do in the NFL—we need our own unique game—but one thing I would like to see the powers that be do is to restrict the bump rule to the first five yards. Right now, you can bump until the ball is in the air. The way people are defending us now, according to NCAA rules, is they're accosting our wide receivers. They're grabbing them, holding them, and decking them. They're not defending the pass; they're just physically restricting what our receivers can do.

I guess that's another way to cater to the pouters.

Before our game against Michigan in 2004, the officials warned their defensive backs about bumping the receivers, so they backed off and played it honest. What happened? We went right down the field on the opening drive and scored. So they changed, and I don't blame them. Lloyd Carr was not going to sit back and watch the Purdue passing game be that productive against the Michigan defense. We had multiple illustrations in that game of defenders grabbing our receivers—and a number of illustrations of receivers, before the ball had been thrown, being knocked down while they were running their routes. None of that was called, and you know why? Because the rules say you can do it. I'm not at all criticizing Michigan. After all, that's what the rules say. They were taking it to the limit, but they were doing what the rules say you can do. And they had the talent to execute it, so more power to 'em. But if we had the NFL rule in effect—and we were able to throw the ball without our receivers being manhandled as they come off the line of scrimmage while mixing in the option game—they'd have to put in some other kind of rule to limit the offense.

We're very comfortable with where we are in this offense today. We actually have begun to recruit guys we think can run the option and also throw the football. We are really making a commitment to move in that direction. We think that's the next phase of the offense. Teams that can throw, run the option effectively, and have a quasi-running back at quarterback will set offensive records.

The extremely gifted, multidimensional quarterback will be the final piece of the puzzle.

Chapter 18

MAXING OUT

I don't mean to say this in an egotistical manner; it's just something that I actually believed. I thought that I was a very good assistant coach—but I thought I would be an even better head coach. I believed that, if I could become a head coach, I would be successful. I thought that for ten years.

I didn't necessarily believe that I would have the opportunity to be a head coach. I wasn't born with a silver spoon in my mouth. I thought, with my pedigree, maybe I was going to be a "lifer" as an assistant. I didn't graduate from a high-profile university; I had not coached at high-profile universities; and I spent nine years in Canada.

When I turned 40, I began to think, instead of being a lifer as an assistant college coach, I should try to position myself to get into the National Football League. I didn't carve it in stone, but I thought, "If I can't become a college head coach before I'm 50, I'm not going to be one." If I would have turned 50 as an assistant, I would have pursued the NFL and given up on college coaching. I was 48 when Paul Roach offered me the Wyoming head coaching job, so I got in under the wire. To be able to realize that dream was an unbelievable happening.

Looking back, I am indebted to Leon Burtnett for hiring me out of Canada, and I'm equally indebted to Paul Roach for offering me a head coaching job.

If you'll recall, I knew that we were leaving Wyoming at halftime of the first game of the 1996 season. It really didn't matter to me where we went. It did, but it didn't, if that makes sense. I took the Purdue job so quickly, who knows what would have happened if I would have delayed just one more week? I do know that Glen Mason and Bob Davie were also candidates for the job. I don't know if Bob or Glen turned down Morgan Burke—or whoever did or didn't say no to him. I also know how that goes. They always say the guy they hire was their first choice, but rarely is that true. With Purdue, it may have been that way, but I'm not positive.

I'm pretty sure they didn't offer the job to Mason, because I know Glen well enough that he would have said, "Hey, they offered me that damn job." It's possible that Purdue wasn't in the ballpark financially to get Glen. I haven't thought much about it,

> "When I went to Wyoming to meet Joe in 1996, we talked about his offense and his interest in the Purdue opening. He said he was comfortable at Wyoming, that he liked the outdoors, and that Purdue was a tough job. So I called Purdue and told them I wasn't sure if this was a fit. I told them, 'The Purdue job is a tough job, and I don't know if they need a cowboy boots-type guy there. I'm not sure that he fits what you want, and I'm not too sure about his offense. I don't mind throwing the ball, but this is quirky.' He didn't sound like a guy who was ready to roll up his sleeves and go to work recruiting against Notre Dame, Michigan, and Ohio State.
>
> "Obviously, I was wrong. I was wrong about him, and I was wrong about the offense. He came across like an easygoing Columbo-type character, but he's much different from that when you actually get to know him. How he treats the press and how he works with his players is much different, so I really didn't get close enough to see the real Joe Tiller."
>
> Gary Danielson

but reflecting back, they probably did offer the job to Bob, because he told me later that he and his wife came to Purdue looking for a house. But he also told me that he had to hang in at Notre Dame because Lou Holtz was leaving. It really doesn't matter. To his credit, Morgan Burke did act very quickly. If he had waited another week, who knows what would have happened? Perhaps we wouldn't be at Purdue today.

I think the quick decision was a combination of two things—I was ready to do something because I knew I was leaving Wyoming, and Morgan had an offer, and he wanted an answer. Despite the fact that Purdue hadn't had a winning season in 12 years, what probably made it an easier decision than going somewhere else was that we had been here before, and we had stayed in touch with Purdue and some of our friends in the community. We had even come back to visit a couple of times, and I had seen some facility changes and knew things were better than when we were here the first time. I thought that maybe we could go to Purdue and have a reasonable degree of success. Although, quite frankly, I didn't think we'd have the success we've enjoyed.

Jim Colletto had announced three games before the end of the season that he was stepping down. The Minnesota media and an Illinois headhunter had contacted me, but those jobs weren't open yet. Instead of sitting back and waiting to see what would happen, the Purdue offer was extended. We'd been there before, so I thought, "Let's do this."

I've had two regrets as a head coach, my first season at Wyoming and then the 2005 season at Purdue.

In 1991 at Wyoming, I think I was too hardnosed. We had kids on that team who had been on Paul Roach's first and second teams with the Cowboys, in 1987 and 1988. They had finished undefeated in the WAC those two years, had finished 10-3 and 11-2 overall, and played in the Holiday Bowl. Some of them felt they were entitled to be on a winning team without necessarily putting in the work. I sensed an attitude that I didn't think would lead to winning, so I really turned the screws hard. My first year as a head coach, I didn't want to be accused of being too soft. We ended up 4-6-1, but I think if I had been a little bit lighter on them, maybe we would have won another game or two. I regret my initial approach. I should have been smarter than that. I guess I was smarter, but I was the new kid on the block, and I wanted to prove a point.

My other regret was the 2005 season at Purdue. If I could do it all over again, I would ignore the media and the fans—all the people who were clamoring about how good we could and should be. As long as I've coached, I had never experienced preseason hype like that. I think, subconsciously, the hype factored into some of the decisions I made. Looking back, I should have dismissed Bernard Pollard after that flare-up in August during training camp. I had kicked a player out of practice for several days before, and it worked. So I did what experience had taught me, but my gut feeling told me I should have canned him; and I didn't.

Maybe when you stop feeling this way you ought to get out of the game, but I felt as though I had a real obligation to not let people down. I didn't want to let the fans down, to be less than what they thought we could be. I allowed some of my thinking to be swayed by what others thought, which is unlike me. I've been a lone ranger over the years—and I am again today. I really don't give a damn anymore. I'm back to the way I used to be. That's why I enjoyed the spring of 2006 as much as any since I've been coaching. I'm relaxed with myself, and I know exactly how I'm going to respond to any situation that challenges our team goals. That's the way it is, and I really don't give a damn about the rest of it.

> "He treats everybody well, whether you're a manager, a trainer, an All-American quarterback or a fifth-string defensive lineman. He's very good with people, has very good people skills. He's fun to be around and has a great sense of humor. But he can be very stern and very firm. He will not budge. He's very stubborn that way. If he believes something is right, that's the way it is. That's made him very good as a head football coach."
>
> Brock Spack

Several times, I've been asked if I think the 2005 season was just a blip on the radar screen; or if our first losing season at Purdue is a sign that the program has slipped and is headed toward a downward spiral.

As we enter the 2006 season, we're probably no different than we've been any other year. We have some issues and some problems, some things we have to address, but that's just part of the challenge of coaching. I think we've addressed some of the major concerns that we had. I couldn't be more pleased with the new coaching staff—impos-

Here I am with most of the family after our 100th win. We beat Ohio State in another comeback victory: (left to right) Arnette, Mike, and Renee. Photo provided courtesy of Purdue University Sports Information

sible to be more pleased with it—and our team has responded accordingly. We're a better team coming out of spring practice 2006 than we were at any time in 2005. Many of them are the same guys, but, as the saying goes, it only takes one bad apple to spoil the barrel. Last season, we had a handful of bad apples, but they've either been eliminated or have eliminated themselves. The ones who remain now understand that there's a new sheriff in town, so to speak. They understand that they're history if they cross the line. So their

"As a coach, he'll allow you to make a mistake. He won't smirk or say I told you so, but when you say, 'Coach, that wasn't the right thing to do, was it?' he'll just say 'Probably not.' When he hired me he told me, 'I'm looking for a guy who will tell me I'm full of crap once in awhile.' He allows us to disagree, but he says, 'I just don't want you to be disagreeable.' You always feel open to say something and to offer suggestions and ideas. If you step out of line, as a coach or a player, he'll let you know, and he'll be very firm and very direct. It's been a great environment to coach in."

Brock Spack

behavior has been different than what it was a year ago. When you combine those two facets, it makes for a better team.

Our string of playing in eight consecutive bowl games was a heck of an accomplishment. We're fortunate that several teams from the same conference can go to a bowl game in college football today. Just think how frustrating it was in the 1960s, when the Boilermakers were so successful under Coach Jack Mollenkopf, but they had to stay home most holidays because the Big Ten champion was the only team going to a bowl game.

For an experienced person in this profession, being involved in bowl games is great. But the more times you make it to a postseason game—I don't want to say there's less excitement—but it's kind of like your first kiss. When you first go to a bowl, you're excited, and many things occur that you have no idea are going to happen. You don't realize how much you're involved in promoting the game and all the activities you are required to attend. And that's fine with me—I don't have any problem with that. That's the way it should be. But I've never really had a great time at any bowl, because it really is intense work for the head coach. You're in the spotlight all the time; you're on call all the time; and you have obligations to promote the game and to manage your own team. During all our bowl game experiences, we've managed to go out to eat as a family just once on each trip. That's not my idea of a relaxing bowl trip. When you go to eight of them in a row and then you don't qualify, from a competitive point of view, it bothers the heck out of you. From a been-there, done-that point of view, it's not that catastrophic when you consider your life's bigger picture.

Going to eight in a row, though, certainly is significant. Purdue was one of only eight programs that were able to string at least eight bowl

> "Joe Tiller is a very pleasant and very able man. He's steady, he's loyal and he's a student of the game. He's rather unflappable. You don't get ol' Joe all tied in a knot very often. He's a family man who loved Wyoming and loved its people. He's trustworthy, opinionated, articulate, fun, and spirited. He's just a good egg."
>
> Alan Simpson
> (Former U.S. Senator from Wyoming)

No matter what happens on the field, our fans are always great.
Photo provided courtesy of Purdue University Sports Information

trips together during that stretch. The list was impressive and included: Michigan, Florida State, Tennessee, Florida, Virginia Tech, Georgia, and Georgia Tech. Obviously, few outfits can manage to make it to eight consecutive bowl games. Purdue, along with Tennessee, will now drop off that list.

Most people would assume that I would consider the Rose Bowl as our crowning achievement, but it's difficult to isolate just one event. Obviously, that event's as high profile as it gets, other than a national championship game. Having grown up in the Midwest, in Big Ten country, the Rose Bowl is the epitome, so it was a great experience to be there, but it probably meant more to other people than it did to me. If we hadn't gone to the Rose Bowl, I still would feel good about what we've accomplished at Purdue. The fact that we went to the Rose Bowl is the icing on the cake.

But I keep coming back to 1997 and 1998. I've just not had any more fun in coaching than I did those two years. If every year could be like '97 and '98, I might coach longer than Joe Paterno. Things have changed so much here at Purdue that there's no chance of that ever happening.

My biggest accomplishment as a head coach is that we've taken two programs that were not high profile and, while our staff was there, both received some national recognition. Our most memorable moment has to be climbing the Ross-Ade Stadium stands after we beat Indiana, Purdue fans celebrating all over the field, to accept the invitation to play in the Rose Bowl. It's hard to top that. I will remember it forever.

"Joe has a way of telling great stories, always with a twinkle in the eye and the bristle of the moustache. That moustache can twinkle too. He's fun, and he needed that sense of humor. I was in politics for 31 years, and he's been in coaching for 35 years—and, man, oh, man, you're the toast of the town one day and toast the next. A good politician and a good coach are very similar. You take your lumps and never let your face show how hard they're kicking your butt."

Alan Simpson
(Former U.S. Senator from Wyoming)

It's more difficult trying to determine our proudest moment. That one's tough because we've had so many teams that have really put it all out there and pulled off tremendous comebacks. We've had teams that never gave up and teams that came back from unbelievable circumstances to win. How can you be more proud of one team over another? My proudest moments would be the multiple times I've been around teams that have had tremendous comeback victories. We've created a culture at Purdue that our teams believe they can win every game they play. They may not win, but they believe they can win every time they take the field.

During our run so far at Purdue, I really feel like we've reached our potential—even in 2005, when I knew we were going to have quarterback issues. I knew we weren't as good at that position as everyone else thought we were. Still, we were two plays in the Northwestern game, two calls that went against us, from winning that game and going to a bowl. Others may choose not to believe that, but it is a fact.

I often tell our coaches, "It can be a lonely life as a head coach." Here I am, once again, the last guy off the practice field. Photo provided courtesy of the Journal-Courier (Lafayette, Indiana)

During our nine seasons at Purdue, I think we've maxed out. In any given year, could we have won one or two more games? Absolutely, but you could say that about any team in America. We also could have lost another game or two in each of those nine seasons. But we've won a lot of games at Purdue that people didn't think we could win.

Even after the 2005 season, I'm not apologetic—we've maximized our opportunities.

Chapter 19

I AM WHO I AM BECAUSE OF ...

MY MOTHER, JOSEPHINE

My mother was the most influential person in my life. Both my parents were extremely honest, but she was unbelievably honest. She had an incredible work ethic—really unlike anybody I've ever known. She was a disciplinarian, but she never carried a grudge. When it was over, it was over. All her nieces and nephews looked up to her, so she was truly the matriarch of the family. Mom was really a unique person who had an uncanny appreciation of common sense.

It's too bad she grew up in her era, because she was smart enough and talented enough to be a college graduate.

MIKE CARMEN AND BOB RITTICHIER

Mr. Carmen was the head football coach at Rogers High School, and Mr. Rittichier was the wrestling coach and a football assistant.

Besides being a coach, Bob was a great guy and an excellent government teacher, and he greatly influenced my decision to major in social science and minor in history.

Mike was a strong man with a good personality. He was an ex-Marine—but he wasn't mean, just tough. He was a Marine in the truly good sense of the word, and a very good man. He's the guy who got me thinking that maybe I might want to be a coach.

JIM SWEENEY

Coach Sweeney's first season as a college head coach was my senior year, and, to this day, he will introduce me as his first captain. He had a huge influence on me—more than anyone in my life, because he was my coach. I had a player-coach relationship and, later, a coach-coach relationship with him. He influenced me in terms of my core beliefs and my philosophy. I think it was good that he came into my life when he did, because those were formative years for me; and he was really a continuation of the way I was raised. When I first started coaching, I found myself coaching the way Jim coached.

Coach Sweeney was a hard-rock miner from Butte, Montana, who lost his father when he was young. He was a Golden Gloves boxing champion who could be an extreme hard ass. Coach Sweeney was a consummate football guy who studied, lived, and breathed football, and he coached his teams to win with discipline and toughness. When he was young, he was extremely hard on everybody around him, including his staff, but he had the ability to garner unbelievable loyalty. Everybody wanted his approval and his blessing. Maybe he was the right kind of guy for the right time. Coaches who were on his staff during his last five years of coaching have told me how he had mellowed, and maybe he did that because that's what you needed to do to coach today's athlete. But if you were part of his early coaching career, you would find it hard to believe that he had mellowed because he was such a crusty, ornery guy. Jim taught me tough love—that you can be hard on guys and still be their friends and be compassionate when interacting with them.

Coach Sweeney had a unique ability to inspire people and a unique ability to humble people. He had the ability to make you feel like you were at the top of Mount Everest or that you were at the bottom of the ocean with the whale dung. To this day, he's the best person I've ever been around in terms of having the ability to flip the switch—to go from the positive to the negative and back.

I've changed with the times, but fundamentally I still coach very much the way he coached me. When I first started out, I was hard-nosed and pretty much walked the line. I've changed some, but I think that your core values and your basic beliefs never change. When you go through tough times you invariably fall back on those beliefs. There's an old coaching cliché—"If you don't stand for something, you'll fall for anything." Certainly, I've adapted to the times.

I study human behavior now more than I study coaching. I'm always looking at things from a management point of view. Today, a head coach is perhaps more of a manager than a coach. You need to manage your squad; you need to manage your staff; and you need to manage the job. When I first became a head coach, I didn't think of myself as a manager—I thought of myself as a coach. Yet, in the last decade, more of my emphasis has been on managing principles than on coaching principles. I try to get players to relax more around me, although I'm okay with the fact that they fear the thought of being summoned to the principal's office.

GARY HOBSON

Gary was the general manager of the Calgary Stampeders during our early years in the CFL. He had exceptional people skills and was a very compassionate guy who was excellent at creating a happy environment. He had a way of bringing things into focus, and he always was prepared to turn a negative into a positive. Gary was involved in putting a franchise together, but he wasn't going to slit his wrist if something went wrong. He was a levelheaded person, and his style and personality rubbed off on me. It takes a while, particularly when you're young, to put things in perspective. Gary was as good as anybody at doing that. When you're around a guy like that for a period of time, you begin to think the way he thinks.

One thing Gary said, though—probably the one thing he said more often than anything else—always rubbed me the wrong way. His philosophy, in reference to our wonderful friends in the media, was, "I don't care what they say about me, as long as they are talking about me." The first few times I heard him say that, I told him I didn't agree with him. I didn't want them saying anything about me that forced me to become defensive. I didn't want to be held in judgment by the media. I would much rather have positive things said than negative ones. But his whole idea was, "You can't sell tickets if you aren't in the news."

THE CANADIAN FOOTBALL LEAGUE

The Canadian game taught me to be proactive. Consider the rules: three-down football with motion toward the line of scrimmage, a running clock at all times, 20 seconds on the play clock. The game was moving fast and moving constantly. My first impression of Canadian football was that it looked like the Katzenjammer Kids—everybody was going in different directions. The CFL game was organized chaos.

But once you get used to that pace, it forces you to think ahead. *Okay, the next time we're in this situation, this is what we're going to do.* Coaching in the CFL was the first time in my career that I had to make an adjustment to the speed of the game. But as a result, I've been very comfortable with one-back spread, wing 'em, sling 'em football. Many guys dabbled with it, but they didn't want to commit because they weren't comfortable. I was okay with hurry up and go—it didn't look that much different to me than the Canadian game.

LEON BURTNETT

Leon was the head coach at Purdue from 1983 to 1986, during my first stay at the university. He hired me out of Canada and gave me a chance to return to the American college game. He is a very compassionate guy who would give you the shirt off his back. His strength is his compassion for his players, particularly his ability to build rapport amongst his minority players.

However, at that time in his life, when he was the head coach at Purdue, Leon was kind of living a dream and almost acting like everything was a dream. I thought his friends influenced him too much. I always thought that Leon was an outstanding assistant who, over time, struggled with the role of being a head coach.

One of the things I learned from Leon—and I've told my coaches this—is that you never publicly want to say, "I don't know what the problem is." He believed that once you said that, the response very easily could be, "If he doesn't know what the problem is, let's get somebody in here who can figure it out." There are times when we all feel that way. No one has all the answers; but to say that publicly can come back to harm you.

Another thing I learned from Leon—both good and bad—was that you didn't want to ask for too many favors. You don't want to go up the food chain too often. You don't want to go to your athletic director all the time to solve your problems, and you really don't want to include the president of the university. You have access to those people if you want it, but if they do something for you and things don't go well, it's much easier for them then to say, "I gave that guy all the help he asked for; and he wasn't successful; so I guess it's time for us to make a change."

Leon actually did that. He asked Dr. Steven Beering, who was the president of Purdue at that time, to intercede on a recruit. Only the president's office could issue the ruling in favor of the football program, and it did. But the recruit ended up not being the type of player everybody had predicted. The administration's reaction was, "Hold it, we jumped through all these hoops for a sub-par athlete? We were under the impression that this guy was going to make the difference between us going to a major bowl or not." And they questioned whether we really had the right leadership in place with the football program.

MIKE PRICE

Like Leon Burtnett, I worked for Mike after coaching with him as assistants for Jim Sweeney. Mike was the head coach at Washington State when we were there in 1989-90. One of the most significant things that Mike's ever said—which I've used in staff meetings since—was, "Nothing is as important to other people as it is to us."

Mike figured if others couldn't get the information we were looking for, then we would go get it ourselves. Mike believed in a chain of command but only to a degree. If someone in the chain dropped the ball, then he wanted to pick that ball up and run with it. Until I was with Mike, I had never been around a weekly academic meeting. When I went to Wyoming, I incorporated that, and we still have Friday morning academic meetings at Purdue. We do that so everybody on the staff is on the same page. If something's not getting done by the person who's responsibile, as a coach and a staff we can try to deal with the problem immediately.

Mike always was into theatrics. I assume he still is today as the head coach of the Miners of the University of Texas-El Paso because I saw a picture of him coming down through the stands at a UTEP game with a miner's axe in his hands.

Our first year at Washington State was unbelievable. In one of our late-week practices before we played the Oregon Ducks, he dressed up like a duck hunter. He had on the full garb—the orange hat, the rubber boots, a shotgun over his shoulder, and a duck call in his mouth. He always came out during the first two minutes of warmups. This time, he came out from the far end of the field, just quacking away with that duck call. He came over to the team and said something like, "I'm going duck hunting Saturday. I heard the Ducks don't have a chance against these Cougars—if the Cougars show up and play the way they're capable of playing." Then he walked off the field, blowing his duck call, and looking up in the sky, as if some ducks were going to fly past.

Another time, before a game against Southern California, he had arranged through the agriculture school or veterinary school, to get somebody to ride a horse onto the practice field. It was supposed to be the Southern Cal mascot, but they had to settle for a gray horse instead of a white horse like USC uses. After Mike gathered the team around him, a guy dressed like Tommy Trojan and waving a sword in the air, came onto the practice field riding that horse. He rode over to the team and began circling the players. Mike started yelling, "Who is this guy? What the hell's going on? These damn Trojans, they're everywhere. We've got to get rid of these guys."

He had borrowed a starter's pistol from the track coach, and he pulled it out and started firing—and half the team hit the ground. You immediately knew which kids grew up in the inner city. They didn't stop to ask questions; they didn't look around to see what it was; they weren't laughing. They heard a gun, and they hit the ground.

Mike did something like that most every week. As I observed him, I thought, "Well, that's Mike Price, but that's not me."

Mike's wife, Joyce, is a very engaging lady, and she always helped in recruiting. I think my wife, Arnette, enjoys doing the same partly because of Joyce.

PAUL ROACH

Paul Roach taught me how to interact with people—from how to relate as a subordinate to how to relate to subordinates.

He also taught me some of the important philosophies of football. One of his beliefs was, "The hay was never in the barn." There's an old belief in football that, by the time Thursday arrives, you can't add anything. I didn't like late changes, so I believed, that the hay *was* in the barn. However, Paul demonstrated that, if you see something late in the week that can help you get a little bit of an edge, you should use it. Paul also had a distinct philosophy about what he wanted to do on the goal line, and he was willing to abandon the one-back style completely at that point.

When you're the athletic director and the head coach, you certainly have to delegate, and he did. But the one thing he always wanted to do was call the plays on Saturday. He loved the strategic part of the game. I learned a lot from him in that department because he often would ask me for input. As a head coach today, I believe in delegating because of him. Until I worked with Paul, I had never been around anyone who delegated the way he did. I wasn't convinced that delegating was the way to go. But I found out that, if you get good people, you should get the heck out of their way and let them do their jobs.

Today, I like trick plays, and I got that from Paul as well. He always was looking for "trickems," as he called them. Even today, when I watch game tape on an opponent, I'm always on the lookout for trick plays because I find that part of the game fun.

Chapter 20

THE HOME TEAM

When I was maybe in my second year of coaching, at Montana State, I was a good friend with Dick Roach, also on that staff. I wasn't married yet, and Dick and his wife, Laverne, would invite me to their house. It was kind of fun to be around their young kids. One day, Laverne asked me what I wanted to be when I grew up. I said, "I'd like to get married and raise a family." With three children of her own, she said, "You've got to have some goals higher than that." I knew it was a simple goal, but that was it. I wasn't even dating Arnette at that time. Because I grew up in a good family environment, I thought, "That's what you do."

I wasn't aware of the demands that a coach with a family would face. The most significant thing about being a coach and raising a family is that you have a good wife. It is so much easier when you marry someone who is truly a coach's wife. She has to be smart; she has to be independent; she has to be a team player; and she has to be supportive of her husband at all times. It really is much more difficult to be a coach's wife than it is to be a coach.

If you're going to be a coach, you need to be upwardly mobile. When coaches take another job, the family stays behind until the end of the school year. They're going to improve the standard of living for the family, but when they leave their wife and kids behind, that's a tough adjustment—and that occurs fairly often. That's what is different from most other professions. When coaches move, it's not as if we move to a different department within the corporation. We move to a different city, state, or part of the country. It can be a pretty traumatic move, and your wife has to be able to hold the family unit together. Arnette truly has excelled at that. When you're getting married, you don't know if your spouse is going to be of that mind-set or not. It's more blind luck than anything else, but it's very critical.

About 25 to 30 years ago, an assistant coach at Idaho by the name of Ed Knecht told me something I've never forgotten. He said, "As a coach, you spend your entire life being a parent to someone else's kid; only to wake up and find out when your career comes to an end that you don't know that much about your own kids." I would agree with that, but I think it's changing. Coaches today interact much more with their families. As a head coach, I've allowed that to happen. During my early days, coaches really didn't have much of a family life because we were consumed with the job. If you weren't, then you weren't dedicated. The head coach dictated part of it, but the other part of it was determined by your desire to excel at your profession.

As a coach, it's very interesting to hear what your children tell other people when asked about their hometown. They're born in one town; they go to school in another town for four years; go to a different one for two years. The next thing you know, they're entering adulthood; and they've never been at once place long enough to say, "That's my hometown." I know where my hometown is—Toledo, Ohio. I grew up there and lived there until I went to college. None of our children can say that.

Coaches today spend more time with their families. The rules—such as the 20-hour-a-week rule, which limits the time you can work with the players—give coaches an opportunity to get away from the job. As an assistant coach, I never went to parent-teacher conferences when the girls were young. I did with Michael, but not with Renee and Julie. Arnette always did that. As I grew older—maybe Knecht's comment created a guilt complex—I attempted to become more involved in their lives. But I had missed a big part of it, except for Christmas and a two-week vacation in the summer. Many, many times, when I came home at night, they were already in bed and the next morning I was gone before they got up. Days would go by without me seeing my children. I'm not saying it's right, but you kind of get used to that.

I would do it all over again, but I would like to do it in today's environment instead of the environment that I worked in. Today, I encourage my staff to attend parent-teacher conferences. In my day, we never would do something like that—we never even thought of it. One thing I did do with Renee, our oldest daughter, was to take her with me on an overnight scouting trip while we were in Calgary. Just the two of us flew to Vancouver (we did accumulate air-travel miles even back then), where I had to scout a game. We shopped a little during the day, and I scouted the game that night. It was fun, but we only got to do it once. Another time, much later, while we were at Washington State, I took our son, Mike, to watch a high school game in Walla Walla, Washington. I had the eastern part of Washington as a recruiting area, and I had to go see a young quarterback by the name of Drew Bledsoe. During the return trip, before Mike fell asleep in the car, he asked me, "Do you think he's as good as Jim Everett?" My response was, "Oh yeah, Mike, I think he'll be even better." We didn't get home until around 1 a.m., but it was fun having him along. Unfortunately, I never had an opportunity to sneak off anywhere with our other daughter, Julie.

Once I became a head coach in today's environment, it was a little different. It was neat that I got to see Julie sing in the high school choir. It was great that I got to see Mike's high school football team in

Laramie win the state championship. That was a unique experience. We were playing at Colorado State that day, and an alum flew me to Mike's game and then flew me back to Fort Collins for our game. The only thing that could have been better that day—given that Mike's team won its game—was if we could have backed that up with a win, but we didn't. Probably under any other conditions, I wouldn't have been able to do that. I'm not sure I would have done that at Purdue, just because everything is so much more visible and high profile. They literally delivered me to the stadium just in time for the game. I went in, put my coaching clothes on, and went out for the warm-ups. Even though we lost that game, no one criticized me or blamed me.

We were living in Calgary when Renee started school. An alley was behind the house we were renting, and on the other side of the alley was a schoolyard with a chain-link fence around it. On her first day of going to school by herself, I gave her a kiss, and she walked out the door, with her coat on and her little lunch bucket in her hand. As she walked away, I thought that I'd lost my little girl forever. Now I'm going to trust someone else with her. It seemed like a long walk across that schoolyard, but I stood there and watched every single step.

When I was in Calgary, every CFL team had an open date during the season. We had a family outing where the wives made picnic lunches, and everybody got together at one of the parks. That was just a ball—to be able to actually do something with your family. That was the first time I can remember doing something as a family during the football season. The coaches still went in to work and watched tape until noon, but then we all checked out and went to the family picnic.

Our kids were pretty good about their situation because Arnette was so involved in their lives and did such a great job of raising them. If there was anything they needed, she was there. When I say, "She raised them," I mean *she raised them.*

Today, it is significantly different than it was 20 years ago.

ARNETTE TILLER—A COACH'S WIFE

I first met Joe when he was coaching at Montana State. I was living with the girlfriend of Cliff Hysel, one of Joe's college teammates. The girls were out partying, and Cliff's girlfriend said, "Go get that Tiller away from Cliff so I can talk to him." So I walked over and dragged Joe onto the dance floor. We danced, and then we sat up and talked all night. Five months later, we were engaged.

I was attracted to Joe because he was pleasant, and he had a really neat car, a 1960 Riviera. He was sort of like the clean-cut Joe College, and I was 180 degrees the other direction—drinking, smoking, carousing, partying, and working for a living. He kind of had this plan for his life and was very meticulous and orderly, and we sort of met in the middle. When we got married in 1967, I was 22; and he was 24.

Although I had been to some football games at my small high school in Belgrade, Montana—about 10 miles west of Bozeman—I knew nothing about the sport. I had never been to a college football game. I was the queen of "ignorance is bliss." I didn't have a clue, so I didn't have any expectations about being the wife of a coach. It didn't take me long to find out that Jim Sweeney was a maniac—in a really good way. He believed that if he was at the office 24 hours a day, his teams would play better. So the coaches wouldn't get home until 1 or 2 in the morning and then go back to work at 7 a.m.

We lived in an apartment for six months, got through the first season, and then we bought our first house. The realtor suggested that we tear it down and build on a foundation that was at the back of the property, but Joe decided that we would try to fix up the house. So we borrowed $1,000, put $500 down, and spent $500 on tools and wood, and started renovating. It was actually a garage that had been turned into a house. We gutted it, laid a foundation, and turned it into a better shack. It was a shack, and then it was a better shack. We lived in that house for three and a half years, affectionately calling it the Sugar Shack. Before the kitchen was done, I had an electric coffee pot,

Arnette being her usual quiet self at our first Alamo Bowl game.
Photo provided courtesy of Purdue University Sports Information

a two-burner hot plate, and an electric frying pan to do all of our cooking. We would put the dirty dishes in a laundry basket and take them to some friends' house to wash them.

One particular winter, we became the picture of eternal optimism, sitting in the living room of the Sugar Shack, freezing to death. We tried to use the stove as a heater, but it wouldn't heat that little house. The snow was blowing so hard it was coming through the cracks in the window. We didn't have a television, so we were sitting there, with our coats on, reading the Gurney Seed Catalogue. That was a brutal winter, something like 20 below for about 37 days. We received a certificate from the local newspaper to prove that we were in town all that time and managed to survive.

During this freeze, the septic tank filled up, all of our plumbing froze, and then the pump froze. We bought an insulated extension cord so we could put a space heater down in the well shaft. When Joe lifted the lid of the well shaft, steam came out. It was frozen inside, so Joe had to dig it out. Finally, I handed him the cord out the window, but every time he unrolled it, the plastic around it would break. It froze so fast that it snapped every time he unrolled it.

One summer Joe was working as a bouncer at a place where my dad tended bar—the Corner Club out at Four Corners. That was his contribution to our income, while I was working at the beauty shop. One day, we were driving home from work; and I had a dime, so I asked Joe if he had a quarter so I could buy a pack of cigarettes. He didn't have a quarter, so he said, "If I don't have a quarter for your cigarettes, can I borrow your dime to buy a newspaper?"

We always moved, even when we weren't changing jobs. In Bozeman, we rented the apartment and then bought the Sugar Shack. At Washington State, we lived in married housing our first year and then moved into a duplex. At that time, the Calgary economy was booming, so we lived in four different houses during our nine years there. Our first stops at Purdue and Wyoming, and then our second stay at Washington State, we lived in just one house each time. After Joe became the head coach at Wyoming, we were in Laramie for six years and lived in three different places. This second time around at Purdue, we've lived in the same house the entire time. We remodeled nine houses while we were living in them—just trying to make a buck when we sold them.

When Joe was on Coach Sweeney's staff at Washington State, they didn't have a recruiting budget, so the coaches couldn't go to the business office and get travel money. They had to go to the bank and borrow money. Then they would get reimbursed and pay their bank loan back, but it was all in the coach's name, not in the school's name. Those were the lean years, the very lean years.

Coach Sweeney was a Marathon Man. The coaches worked all day, every day; all night, every night; seven days a week. You had to get permission to call in sick, or be half dead to have a meal at home. If Joe's parents came to town for a game, that was tough. They didn't see him except on the field on game day.

A couple of coaches' families lived in a row of duplexes, and, of course, there were a bunch of little kids. We would joke that the neighbors probably thought we were the unluckiest prostitutes in the world—because these car lights came in late at night, but when the neighbors got up in the morning, there were no cars. We were just there with a bunch of little kids.

When Joe went to work for the Calgary Stampeders, it wasn't a big deal for me. Having been raised in Montana, our family would go back and forth to Canada, so it was never like being in a foreign country. But moving to Canada was a little different. We went in as landed immigrants, because we had children in school, and we didn't want to be on a sixth-month visa where we'd have to leave the country in the winter. We had to petition the government to acquire landed-immigrant status, which gave us some rights, such as the ability to buy land, and we could receive some government benefits, such as their socialized medicine; but we couldn't vote.

When we moved to Canada, our two daughters, Renee and Julie, were six and four years old. Our son, Michael, was born in Canada, and that later caused a bit of a problem.

We wrongly assumed that being U.S. citizens meant that he would be a U.S. citizen, but a child is a citizen of the country in which he is born unless the parents register him with the homeland within six months. When we were getting ready to move back to the U.S.—after Joe was hired as an assistant at Purdue—Michael was five. He was not a U.S. citizen, and there was some question about us being able to take a Canadian citizen across the border with us. I had to spend a few hours applying for U.S. citizenship for that child so he could come home with us.

The time we've spent in Indiana, four years back in the '80s and these past 10 years, is the only time I haven't lived in the West. I actually became a college student at Purdue in 1984 at the age of 40. I had to take the Scholastic Aptitude Test to be accepted and majored in art education. As it turned out, I studied two years at Purdue, two years at Wyoming, two years at Washington State, and the final two years at Wyoming. It took me eight years to earn a bachelor's degree in art.

When we went from Laramie to Washington State (for our second stay in Pullman), Michael was in junior high, but Renee and Julie both were out of high school, and they didn't want to move. That first Thanksgiving, Julie decided she wanted to move from Laramie to Pullman, so we borrowed my sister's utility trailer and spent Thanksgiving weekend driving to Wyoming, loading her stuff, and taking her back to Pullman. The next fall, Renee decided she wanted to move from Denver to Pullman. So we borrowed the utility trailer, again at Thanksgiving time, drove to Denver, packed up her stuff, and drove back to Pullman. Two weeks later, Joe was hired as the head coach at Wyoming, so Renee didn't even get to unpack.

Things happen all the time that indicate how little most people understand about a coach's life—what they do and the commitment involved. One time, my nephew from Chicago came to a Purdue game and brought a friend with him. While he was here, he wanted to know if Joe and I were going to attend a White Sox playoff game. When I told him that there wasn't time, he wanted to know why Joe couldn't take a day off during the week. A day off? Not from August 1 to February 1—on a good year. And when you say that coaches don't get a day off, people think they work from eight to five. There's just no concept. I know there now are many overpaid coaches, but years ago, if you figured out an hourly wage for a coach who was earning $100,000 a year, he was getting paid maybe two dollars an hour.

When the kids were smaller, and we were at bowl games in December, they were upset because they weren't having the home and hearth, family Christmas, with the tree and the presents. But now that they're older, they remember the Christmas when we were the only people at the San Diego Zoo and the Christmas when we went horseback riding in the Arizona desert. And they are okay with it all.

The kids love what their father does, and they love the football, but they hate being known. When we're at bowl games, they don't even want to walk down the street with us, or walk across the hotel lobby with us. They want to meet us at the car, because they don't like all the handshaking and the hero worshipping.

It's definitely not easy being the son or daughter of a football coach. One time when we were in Wyoming, Michael was in the fifth grade and went out for recess. They were playing football, and one of the kids just creamed him. And then he stood over him and said, "You're dad must be an awful football coach because you're an awful football player."

Joe made it to two of Renee's high school volleyball games, but he never made it to any of Julie's games. It's different now. The coaches will miss something regarding coaching and go to those events. Joe has learned from experience, and he's good about allowing time for the coaches and their families. Yet, when our kids were little, it was not an option.

We always tried to have a life and then showed up on Saturday to enjoy his. When we first got married, I'd watch those wives who were too involved in what their husbands were doing, and they were miserable.

Right after we were married, Joe would come home and be very demonstrative. I actually told him that he could either stay at work or leave it at work, but I wasn't spending my life walking on eggshells—and we didn't. If we had a game and the kids wanted to have a sleepover that night, we had a sleepover that night. To Joe's credit, despite the long hours and the pressures of the job, he's been very good about not bringing it home with him.

RENEE TILLER

Strangely, even though my parents are not divorced and actually have a strong marriage, at times growing up it felt like a single-parent home because my father was gone so much of the time. I often joke that they are horrible role models for me because they've set such high relationship standards.

However, when my dad was at home, it was great quality time. He really made the effort. As you can tell by his interviews and radio show, my father is really quite funny. I want him to know this is the first time I have admitted that. As a child, you just think your parents aren't cool. Looking back, he had his moments.

Because of his work and travel schedules, our "good nights" were often over the phone. I can remember playing a game with him. I would say, "I love you more," then he would say, "No, I love you more." We would go back and forth. He was very patient with it, and it would go on for quite awhile.

When I was about eight, he woke us all up very early, very excited and hyping a new car that we had just received. We were hustled outside. It was a freezing morning in April in Calgary, and we were in our slippers and pajamas. April Fools!

I was in the fifth grade when he took me on a father-daughter trip to Vancouver, British Columbia. It was a working weekend for him, but I was away with my dad, and I felt very grown up. It was very special to me.

I attended Catholic grade schools. Puberty, public school, and rebellion all hit at the same time. We were in the small town of Cochrane, Alberta, with a small church. I was attending a retreat, and our parents were asked to write letters for us to open while we were there. I expected one from Mom but was surprised to see there was a separate one from Dad. I was brought to tears at the realization of how well he knew me, as well as the depth of pride and high expectations for me.

My mom, thank goodness, is a wonderful woman. She went to every single one of our events, worked at our schools, and volunteered whenever she could. She really made up the difference. The whole time we were growing up we were never told there was anything we couldn't do. A good example was roofing the garage. Your dad needs help. You want to help? Need a boost? If we wanted to do something, our parents would scrimp and make sacrifices themselves to make it happen.

Being the established tomboy in the family, I resented when my little brother, the only boy, was old enough to take my place playing catch. Then Dad and Mike started going to Saturday breakfast—just the boys. Ouch! Now Mike and I are more alike than either of us cares to admit and are the best of friends.

As for perks, I have to say that I know more about football than most men I have met and have a genuine love of college football. There are a lot of opportunities that were created for me because of my father's success. Unfortunately, being the independent person

Man's best friend—our golden retriever of 11 years, Millie, who's always glad to see me, win or lose.
Photo provided courtesy of Purdue University Sports Information

that I am, I did not always recognize what was in front of me or was put off by thinking it was Daddy's opportunity, not mine.

The bowl games were great. Spending Christmas with 100 college age men is hard to beat. I walked into the dining room for Christmas dinner at a Holiday Bowl and told my mom, "Now that is what I call a room with a view."

Because of his profession, I have been able to travel to all but three states, plus Mexico and Canada. It was also to my benefit that he has been dealing with teenagers all those years. A lot of what I got into he had already encountered with his players.

The negative—I have gotten into heated arguments with "fans" for having the nerve to talk about my father. People expect you to second-guess your dad's choices, plays, etc. I frequently play the dumb-girl card just to avoid confrontation or just to avoid the stupid people who think they could do better.

Staying on the move has made long-term relationships scarce, but overall it has been a pretty good life.

JULIE TILLER

My dad loved to scare the crap out of us. When I was about 14 or 15, and he was an assistant at Purdue, our house on Old Farm Road had a big bay window in the back room. Six of my girlfriends were over for a sleepover, and we were all gathered together in the corner of this sectional, because we were watching one of those good, ol' horror flicks, complete with axe murderer.

Without us knowing it, my dad put on an old, distorted Halloween mask, put his robe on backwards, slipped out the front door, and snuck around back. He waited in the bushes by the bay window for the axe murderer to appear in the movie. As the music in the movie was building, he knocked on the back window, screaming his head off. Some girls literally wet their pants. They never came back to our house again.

I was very shy, and changing from school to school was very hard. I attended three high schools—Central Catholic and Jefferson in Lafayette, and Laramie High School. No matter where we went, Mom made us join at least one extracurricular activity in order to meet people and be a part of things.

When we went to Wyoming, right after I turned 16, I thought it was the end of the world. We had lived in Lafayette for four years, and I had just established all my friends. All of a sudden, my parents said, "Now we're moving to Wyoming." I was wondering, "Do they even drive cars there?"

Moving to Wyoming at that age seemed like the worst thing that I had ever gone through in my entire life. I sat in the back of the Jeep, crying for 1,200 miles. But 10 years later, when my parents told me that dad was going to be the head coach at Purdue, and we were moving back to Indiana, I was like, "Buh-bye, now—have fun. I ain't leaving Wyoming."

Let's see, mountains or cornfields?

When we moved to Wyoming the first time, the people there were very standoffish and cliquish in the beginning. One time, a kid was taunting me until he found out that my dad coached for Wyoming—and he thought that was just the coolest thing. I told him, "Yeah, but you get to grow up with a dad—and I got free tennis shoes." (Due to my father's shoe contracts, all of us received free tennis shoes.)

Actually, in comparing Wyoming and Purdue, it was easier to do things as a family at Wyoming. Soon after my father was hired as Purdue's head coach and they moved to West Lafayette, the two of us were shopping at Sears, and this guy literally stalked us as we walked around the store. From aisle to aisle, we'd see him peak around corners—"Yeah, that's him, the Purdue coach, and he's in Sears; and he's shopping for tools."

When we would be driving, people would roll down their windows and wave at us. In Laramie, we would go to the grocery store or go out to dinner, and the people just kind of accepted you for who you were, and you'd go on your merry way. There wasn't any celebrity aspect. To me, dad wasn't a celebrity. I grew up with this guy who's as normal as can be, a guy who'd love to live in a hardware store if he could.

I am tremendously proud of my father, knowing what he went through to get where he is, and I enjoyed it all—going to the bowl games and enjoying his success through him.

My favorite bowl game experience is not the Granddaddy of Them All. The Rose Bowl is too stuffy. The Rose Bowl was a nice experience, but you don't get to have much fun because of the required functions. You can't go out on the town and just hook one on because someone might see you. The Rose Bowl is similar to the situation at Purdue. We call the fans at Purdue, "the tennis people." They wear their Dockers and their little Duck shoes, and when they're watching football they just sit there, clap, and yell at you to sit down. "If you want to sit down, go watch tennis," I tell them. "This is a football game, get on your feet, do some cheering, let them know you're here."

In Pasadena, it was the redcoats and the very prim and proper. At the Sun Bowl, they drop you off at a bar; and you ride a bull, and you sing karaoke. That atmosphere was more to my liking. I felt comfortable there.

But I have to admit, the shining moment for Dad, as far as I'm concerned, was probably after we beat Indiana to clinch the Rose Bowl berth. I sat at my house in Wyoming listening to the game on the computer, crying in the hallway by myself. I listened to his comments on the field after the game. To hear the pride, to hear his voice crack, to hear him be so happy—I couldn't help but cry.

The older I got, the more I realized that my father did know what was happening in my life and thought about us, but most of the time, he was just that silent man who came home and ate dinner, went to bed, woke up, and went back to work. When I was younger, I didn't think he even knew we existed. One time, when we were at Washington State, he gave a speech to a bunch of other coaches, and Mom came home in tears. I thought, "Great, what the hell happened now?"

"He finally got it," she said. "He was talking to these coaches about their careers and he told them the one thing they needed to remember most was their family, because he has two daughters, one who's 20 and one who's 18, and he has absolutely no idea who they are."

One of my favorite stories about my dad is when somebody asks him what he's going to do when he retires. He usually smiles and says, "Well, I'm going to buy me an RV. I'm going to start up north and travel south because it'll get warmer as we go through the fall. I'm just going to pull in somewhere, and I'm going to throw the best tailgate party ever. And then, when the game starts, I'm going to go into my RV, and I'm going to take a nap. Because, Lord knows, I've seen enough damn football games. When the game's over, I'm going to come out and continue with the tailgate party."

The majority of the time I spend with my father is in silence. We just sit on the porch in Wyoming, where my parents are going to retire, have our beer, and stare at the owls and the wild turkeys—just knowing each of us is there. I learn a lot about my father by listening to the stories that he tells people.

To this day, I don't know very much about my father, and I can't wait for him to retire so that I can get to know him.

MIKE TILLER

It was tough as a kid because Dad was away from home so much, but when he did have time, he went out of his way to spend it with us. He volunteered to be an assistant coach for our baseball team, even though he might have gone to only five practices that whole season. It wasn't that he didn't want to be there, he just couldn't be there. I'm sure every single coach's kid would say the same thing. The schedule is absolutely brutal. But there are benefits. It's an absolute dream for any kid to get to hang around a locker room before and after a game. And to be on the sideline was just amazing.

My absolute favorite moments as a kid were when the staff got together after the games and would watch the ESPN night game or some other game on television. Those guys were absolutely hilarious. The way they watched a game was like a musician listening to a recording.

It was really rough at Wyoming. As small a community as Lafayette is, if you cut that down to just a quarter, that's Laramie. Back then, Wyoming was kind of like Purdue is now. Despite the limitations that are inherent with the job, they really do expect you to play at a championship level every single year. In Wyoming, it was just brutal because there was no way to escape it. Our house was egged after a playoff loss to Brigham Young in my dad's last game at Wyoming— perhaps because they were more upset he was leaving than because of the loss. That team was the first-ever Top 25 team and the first-ever 10-win team in the history of Division I football that didn't go to a bowl game.

A definite highlight for me was when my father came to my state championship football game when we were at Laramie. We were unde-feated my senior season, and we were in Casper playing for the state title—at what is now called Dick Cheney field. Our game was an afternoon game, and Wyoming was playing later at Colorado State. Dad traveled with the team on Friday, and the next day a booster flew him to Casper to watch our game. And then he flew back. We won the game, and it was really neat that he made the effort to be there for it. That was pretty special.

Our most recent family photo. Sitting in front is Mike, with one of our golden retrievers, Patty. I'm next to our other golden, Millie. Standing (left to right) are Renee, Julie, with her husband, Jason; and Arnette.
Photo provided courtesy of Purdue University Sports Information

It's hard to be the new kid once in your life, let alone every two to four years. I was very fortunate to be born in Canada, where I lived on some acreage with some cows and horses. Although in the same sense, even today, I really don't feel at home anywhere. When people ask me where I'm from, I don't know what to say. I generally tell them "Wyoming," but sometimes I say, "Canada."

One of my fondest memories with Dad was in 1993 or 1994 at Wyoming. My mom had a Christmas party for the St. Laurence choir. While they were very nice people, the party wasn't exactly my dad's cup of tea. So he and I closed ourselves in my room and played a game where one of us would name a school and the other person had to guess the nickname. We did that for two or three hours. Mom jokes about how she nearly divorced Dad for that. Little did I know that one of my favorite memories is not one of hers.

I have so many reasons to be proud of my dad. But perhaps the thing I admire most about him is his dedication. I just can't imagine anybody working harder or doing it any better than he does.

FOURTEEN FOR THE BOOKS

When you've been in the coaching profession as long as I have, you experience both the thrill of victory and the agony of defeat many times. You're on the sideline for many outstanding, and strange, games.

I've been asked many times about the most memorable games in which I've coached, but, while trying to come up with a Top 10 list, I discovered that it's no easy task. So here is a list of 14 most memorable games, the first five as an assistant and the last nine as a head coach.

Montana State 29 - Montana 24
November 2, 1968—at Montana

The Montana-Montana State rivalry once was covered in the *New Yorker* magazine as one of the top five college rivalries outside of Division I.

This was Tom Parac's first game against the Grizzlies as Montana State's head coach, after Jim Sweeney had left for Washington State. We had a senior quarterback named Dennis Erickson, who later went on to coach Miami to a national championship and then to coach Seattle and San Francisco in the NFL. We were favored going in, and we jumped out to a 9-0 lead in the second quarter. The Grizzlies scored the next 24 points—10 in the second quarter and 14 in the fourth quarter—to take a 24-9 lead with only eight minutes left to play. But we scored three touchdowns in those eight minutes to pull out an exciting victory.

We finished with 533 yards, the first time in school history that Montana State finished with more than 500 total yards. Erickson had an outstanding game—with 23 completions in 39 attempts for 282 yards and two touchdowns—and Ron Bain caught 12 passes for 152 yards and two TDs.

Yet, the player of the game ended up being sophomore running back Paul Schafer, who was merely 5-foot-10 or so and 175 pounds. Despite playing with a separated shoulder, incredibly he carried 58 times for 234 yards—both school records—and two touchdowns, including the game-winner on a one-yard run with only 12 seconds remaining. After the game, that kid's body was a sight to behold. He had some skin scraped off one rib, and a hip pointer on the opposite side, and his shoulder had been shot up. It was just an unbelievable performance in a heck of a game.

Washington State 52 - Washington 26

November 24, 1973—at Washington

As a coach, you don't have very many games when everything goes right for your team and everything goes wrong for the opponent. That's what happened in this game. Unbelievably, we went off the field at halftime with a 42-6 lead—and we were the underdogs coming into the game.

In the locker room, head coach Jim Sweeney told the coaches, "We play these guys every year, and we know they're damn good, so we better rein this in a little bit."

I spoke up and said, "Bullshit to that. We need as many points as we can get against these guys."

Sure enough, Washington came out and outscored us 20-0 in the third quarter, but we woke up in the final quarter and held on for the victory.

That game's beginning made it very memorable. Rivalry games almost never go that way. I had seen it happen before but when I was on the other sideline.

Purdue 23 - Notre Dame 21
September 8, 1984—The Hoosier Dome

The very first game played in the Hoosier Dome, this was really a Notre Dame home game, and they were heavy favorites. It was kind of a coming-out game for our quarterback, Jim Everett, who completed 20 of 28 passes for 255 yards and two touchdowns.

I was the defensive coordinator and coached the defensive front. Going into the game, our staff had decided—because we had an undersized defense—that we had to rotate and we had to substitute. If we had played just our starting front four, they wouldn't have had anything left by the end of the game. So every other series, I rolled 'em.

Late in the third quarter, Notre Dame was driving, and, all of a sudden, head coach Leon Burtnett came running up the sideline to me, took the headset away from my ear, and said, "What in the hell are those guys doing out there?" It was our second team that the

Fighting Irish were driving against, and he didn't think they should be in the game. I said, "It's their turn, Coach." Fortunately, Notre Dame didn't score on that drive. As it turned out, we finished the game with our No. 1 unit on the field, stopped the Irish, and ended up winning.

The environment, the fact that we were the heavy underdog, and the way the game played out made it unforgettable.

Purdue 17 - Indiana 15
November 22, 1986—at Purdue

This was Leon Burtnett's final game as Purdue's head coach and my last game as an assistant for the Boilermakers. But that's not why this game made the list—it's because of Rod Woodson's incredible performance. We had already been fired, and we made the decision to let Rod play both ways. We had toyed with that idea in the past but always felt like the offense would take away from his effectiveness on defense, and always decided that it wasn't worth it. But this time we thought, "Hey, this is our last game here; we're not coming back next year." We didn't really care if it proved to be a poor strategy—it became, "Let's just see what happens."

Of course, the guy had maybe the most outstanding performance ever by a Purdue player. Against the Hoosiers, Woodson was on the field for 137 plays. On offense, he rushed 15 times for 93 yards and caught three passes for 87 yards. At his regular position as a safety on defense, he finished with 10 tackles, caused a fumble, and broke up a pass. On special teams, he returned three punts and two kickoffs.

Plus, it was an exciting day because we went out to warm up in our usual black home jerseys but then changed into special gold jerseys for the game. They were a dirty gold and pretty ugly. But when the team ran on the field for the start of the game the crowd exploded.

Visiting with all-time great Rod Woodson. Photo provided courtesy of the Journal-Courier (Lafayette, Indiana)

Wyoming 48 - Air Force 45
September 24, 1988—at Air Force

To this day, this is still one of the most exciting games I've ever been around, and it's still talked about as one of the great games in Wyoming history. It was one of those seesaw games. It seemed like every time we would score, Air Force would come back with a score. We never could distance ourselves from them. It came down to the last series, and our freshman kicker, Sean Fleming, kicked a game-winning field goal as time expired.

Air Force had a heck of a quarterback named Dee Dowis. He was a real magician with the option, and he ended up making a number of All-America teams. On this day, Dowis rushed 27 times for 208 yards and two touchdowns. But our quarterback, Randy Welniak—who had to make the switch from being a Wishbone quarterback to being a passing quarterback—completed 28 of 43 passes for 359 yards and three touchdowns. Plus, he rushed 11 times for 108 yards and a touchdown.

Air Force rushed 61 times for 437 yards; and we passed 43 times for 359 yards. When all was said and done, we had 571 total yards, and they had 478 yards. It was truly a track meet. Of the 93 points, 66 were scored in the second half. Wyoming was trailing 38-17 heading into the fourth quarter, but the Cowboys outscored Air Force 31-7 the rest of the way. What an unbelievable game.

San Jose State 26 - Wyoming 24
October 3, 1992—at Wyoming

This was only my second season as a head coach. San Jose State's coach was Ron Turner, and its quarterback was Jeff Garcia. But even more important, it had a kicker by the name of Joe Nedney, who's still kicking in the NFL for the San Francisco 49ers.

We took the lead, 24-23, with 34 seconds left in the game. But then they returned the kickoff and got a couple of first downs. There were two seconds on the clock, and they used their final timeout to set up a 60-yard field goal attempt. After they lined up, we called a time-out to try to ice Joe. After prancing around during that timeout, Joe lined up again, but we called our last timeout.

Finally, Joe Nedney lined up and kicked that ball—dead center—and it sailed five yards above the crossbar. He could have kicked it from 65 yards out. He nailed that thing. That was one of the most helpless feelings I've ever had as a coach. A 60-yarder? C'mon.

One of the things that was unique about playing in Laramie was that I couldn't tell you how many times I would be talking to the visiting coach before the game, and his kicker would come by and say, "I'm good from 50 today coach."

Kickers loved that 7,200-feet elevation.

Wyoming 17 - San Diego State 6
November 7, 1992—at Wyoming

Because of legendary running back Marshall Faulk, San Diego State was receiving a lot of national attention, and this game was televised regionally by ABC—something we didn't get very often. Bo Schembechler, the great former Michigan coach—complete with black cowboy hat—rode into Laramie and was the network's color analyst.

We played a great game, and our defense did a great job against Faulk. He ended up with 33 carries for 127 yards. He also had four receptions, so it wasn't like we totally shut him down, but we kept him out of the end zone, and that was the big thing. We played a great defensive game against a very explosive offense. It probably helped that the weather was bad, with heavy snow and strong winds. Both teams ended up with exactly the same amount of rushing yards, 139. We only threw the ball 35 times and finished with 266 yards—both of which were very low for us at the time.

I think Bo was proud of us because we played what would be described as "… a low-scoring, defensive, Big Ten kind of game."

Wyoming 32 - Fresno State 28
October 30, 1993—at Wyoming

This was a big game because I was able to beat my mentor, Jim Sweeney. Both teams were having great seasons. They had a heck of a team with Trent Dilfer at quarterback.

It snowed heavily that week. The snow was graded off the field, up against a chain-link fence, probably four feet high, just outside the end zones. Fresno State got up big early, but we scored three consecutive touchdowns, including one with 20 seconds left, to take a 32-28 lead. In the final seconds, Fresno State was driving for the winning touchdown, and Dilfer threw a pass in the back of the end zone. But Steve Hendrix, our 5-foot-11, 165-pound defensive back, deflected the ball to preserve the victory. At the end of the play, he slipped on that snow bank and hit the top of a post of that chain-link fence. It came under his facemask and knocked out four teeth—two on the top and two on the bottom—and broke his jaw. He was a tough kid, though, and he came back and played later that season.

There is now a rubberized pad, about a foot in diameter and slit in half, draped over the top of that fence.

Wyoming 25 - Colorado State 24
November 16, 1996—at Colorado State

While Purdue and Indiana play for the Old Oaken Bucket, Wyoming and Colorado State play for the Bronze Boot. This was a huge game because we had to come from behind to win the first-ever Pacific Division title after the WAC had expanded to 16 teams.

We had them 13-0 at halftime, and we were feeling pretty good. We felt so good, in fact, that they proceeded to come out and score 24 points in the third quarter while holding us scoreless. We came back to score with nine minutes to go but failed on a two-point conversion attempt, so we were still trailing, 24-19.

Our final drive took place in what was probably the heaviest snow during any game I coached at Wyoming. We drove 96 yards in 14 plays—which took 6:17—and scored on a six-yard run with 1:48 remaining to win the game.

Wide receiver Marcus Harris had an unbelievable performance that day for the Cowboys. It probably won him the Biletnikoff Award, which is presented annually to the nation's outstanding receiver. Harris finished the day with 16 receptions for 191 yards. We completed 30 passes, and he caught more than half of them. He also had three catches during that final drive, and each was on third down to move the chains.

This was my last regular-season game as Wyoming's head coach, and we came from behind to beat a good team, on the road, in a snowstorm, on the last drive of the game.

Purdue 28 - Notre Dame 17
September 13, 1997—at Purdue

This was my first victory as Purdue's head coach, and I'd have to rank it as my most memorable game. We were coming off a shocking loss at Toledo—a very inauspicious beginning for our program. And then we had to turn around and play the Fighting Irish, who were ranked No. 12 and who had won 11 consecutive games against the Boilermakers.

We were clinging to a 14-10 lead at halftime. After a scoreless third quarter, we made it 21-10 with 8:37 to play when Adrian Beasley scored on a 43-yard fumble return. After Notre Dame scored with 1:47 on the clock to close to within 21-17, the Irish tried an onside kick, but we recovered. Three plays later, we clinched the victory when Kendall Matthews scored on two-yard run with 1:02 remaining. Purdue quarterback Billy Dicken had a great day passing, completing 26 of 38 for 352 yards.

Our student section is loud—and very creative.
Photo provided courtesy of Purdue University Sports Information

We were such decided underdogs that, looking back, I think that victory really jumpstarted our program, and that's why it's my most memorable game.

Purdue 22 - Michigan State 21

November 8, 1997—at Purdue

Without a doubt, this was one of the wildest endings I'd ever seen, as the Boilermakers overcame an 11-point deficit in the final 2:13 to win.

It all started when Leo Perez blocked a 39-yard field goal attempt by the Spartans, and Rosevelt Colvin returned it 62 yards for a touchdown. We failed on a two-point conversion attempt, but

John Reeves managed to recover an onside kick for us. We drove down the field, and Edwin Watson scored on a three-yard run with 40 seconds remaining. We failed on another two-point conversion attempt, so the Spartans had a final chance to win it, but Chris Gardner missed a 43-yard field goal attempt with three seconds on the clock.

Our chances of winning were slim to none. Many of the fans were leaving the stadium and came back in. For us to block a kick, return it for a touchdown, recover an onside kick, and score is almost unfathomable.

Purdue 37 - Kansas State 34

December 29, 1998—at San Antonio

This was our second season and second bowl game at Purdue, both in the Alamo Bowl. Kansas State had been ranked No. 1 in the country until it lost in the Big 12 Conference championship game. We were surprised, as were the Wildcats, that they had slipped down to the Alamo Bowl and weren't invited to a New Year's Day bowl.

We were leading 30-20 midway through the fourth quarter, but then Kansas State scored two touchdowns, the second with 1:24 remaining, to take a 34-30 lead. But Drew Brees drove Purdue 80 yards, capping an unbelievable comeback with a 24-yard touchdown pass to Isaac Jones with only 30 seconds left to play.

Despite the final score, both teams struggled offensively, with Kansas State finishing with 308 yards and Purdue with only 235. Brees completed 25 of 53 passes for 230 yards and three touchdowns (and three interceptions).

Kansas State had a great team. Obviously, I remember that final throw, but what I remember most is how well we played on defense. That might have been the best game we played defensively against a quality offense. The Wildcats were ranked No. 4 in the nation coming into that game.

Purdue 31 - Ohio State 27
October 28, 2000—at Purdue

After throwing his fourth interception of the day, which set up a two-yard touchdown run that gave the 12th-ranked Buckeyes a 27-24 lead with 2:16 to play, Drew Brees came back to complete what many Purdue fans now simply refer to as "The Pass." He found Seth Morales behind the Ohio State secondary, and Morales caught the ball in stride and raced into the end zone to complete a 64-yard scoring play with 1:55 on the clock. That exciting victory kept alive our Rose Bowl hopes; and, despite losing at Michigan State the following week, we clinched the trip to Pasadena by closing out the regular season with a victory over Indiana.

Brees completed 39 of 65 passes for 455 yards, with three touchdowns and four interceptions. For just the second time in school history, Purdue had three 100-yard receivers in one game. Vinny Sutherland had 10 catches for 142 yards, Morales finished with seven for 115, and tight end Tim Stratton ended up with 12 for 100.

While this was a dramatic victory, I don't rank it No. 1 because it didn't guarantee us anything. It was a critical game because we needed it to go to the Rose Bowl, but it didn't send us to Pasadena. What pleased me the most was that Drew was able to redeem himself. What a great competitor he was!

A "super hero." One of a popular series of cartoon animations that are shown on the Jumbotron in Ross-Ade Stadium. Photo provided courtesy of Hall of Music Productions, Purdue University

Purdue 35 - Minnesota 28 (OT)

September 29, 2001—at Minnesota

This game was similar to the 1997 Michigan State game in that we managed to win in a very improbable fashion. We were trailing 28-25 with only 19 seconds remaining in regulation—and we were pinned on our 3-yard line with no timeouts. But quarterback Brandon Hance passed 27 yards to John Standeford and then 39 yards to Taylor Stubblefield. With the ball at the Minnesota 31-yard line, the field-goal unit rushed onto the field, and center John Shelbourne snapped the ball to holder Ben Smith with one second remaining—and Travis Dorsch kicked a 48-yard field goal as time expired. We ended up winning in overtime when Hance threw a 19-yard touchdown pass to Standeford, and then Stuart Schweigert intercepted a Minnesota pass in the end zone.

Things eventually didn't work out for Hance at Purdue, and he transferred to Southern California, but he had a career game against the Golden Gophers. He completed 22 of 36 passes for 306 yards and three touchdowns, rushed 13 times for 70 yards—and caught a 31-yard TD pass from tailback Montrell Lowe.

For us to be able to do what we did in those final 19 seconds of regulation is amazing. I wasn't surprised that we won in overtime because our guys were so fired up after kicking that field goal that we weren't going to be denied.

TILLER AT A GLANCE

PURDUE'S BIG TEN AND
NATIONAL RANKINGS UNDER TILLER

(Bowl games included beginning with 2002 season)

Passing offense

Year	Yards per game	Big Ten	NCAA
1997	281.5	1	13
1998	331.5	1	7
1999	328.0	1	4
2000	312.5	1	6
2001	204.2	9	72
2002	255.7	2	31
2003	224.0	4	51
2004	321.2	1	4
2005	241.7	4	36

Total offense

Year	Yards/game	Big Ten	NCAA
1997	459.6	1	7
1998	457.0	2	16
1999	456.0	1	8
2000	471.2	2	4
2001	306.1	11	105
2002	452.2	1	7
2003	372.9	5	65
2004	446.5	2	13
2005	428.5	5	25

TILLER'S RECORD AS A HEAD COACH

Year	School	Overall	Conference (Finish)
1991	Wyoming	4-6-1	2-5-1 (T6th)
1992	Wyoming	5-7	3-5 (T7th)
1993	Wyoming	8-4	6-2 (T1st)
1994	Wyoming	6-6	4-4 (T5th)
1995	Wyoming	6-5	4-4 (6)
1996	Wyoming	10-2	7-1 (1, Pacific Division)
1997	Purdue	9-3	6-2 (T2nd)
1998	Purdue	9-4	6-2 (4)
1999	Purdue	7-5	4-4 (T6th)
2000	Purdue	8-4	6-2 (T1st)
2001	Purdue	6-6	4-4 (T4th)
2002	Purdue	7-6	4-4 (T5th)
2003	Purdue	9-4	6-2 (T2nd)
2004	Purdue	7-5	4-4 (T5th)
2005	Purdue	5-6	3-5 (8)

Wyoming (6 years) 39-30-1 (.564) 26-21-1 (.552)
Purdue (9 years) 67-43 (.609) 43-29 (.597)
Overall (15 years) 106-73-1 (.592) 69-50-1 (.579)

TILLER'S BOWL RECORD

Season	Bowl	Results
1993	Copper Bowl	Kansas State 52, Wyoming 17
1997	Alamo Bowl	Purdue 33, Oklahoma State 20
1998	Alamo Bowl	Purdue 37, Kansas State 34
1999	Outback Bowl	Georgia 28, Purdue 25 (OT)
2000	Rose Bowl	Washington 34, Purdue 24
2001	Sun Bowl	Washington State 33, Purdue 27
2002	Sun Bowl	Purdue 34, Washington 24
2003	Capital One Bowl	Georgia 34, Purdue 27 (OT)
2004	Sun Bowl	Arizona State 27, Purdue 23

TILLER'S RESUME

Given name: Joseph H. Tiller
Date of birth: December 7, 1942
Hometown: Toledo, Ohio
Education: Rogers High School, Toledo, Ohio, 1960; B.S., Secondary
Education, Montana State, 1965
Playing Career: Offensive tackle, Montana State, 1960-63; offensive
lineman, Calgary Stampeders (CFL), 1964
Family: Wife, Arnette; daughters, Renee and Julie; son, Mike

Coaching experience

1965-70	Montana State, Assistant
	(Offensive and defensive lines)
1971-73	Washington State, Assistant
	(Offensive coordinator/offensive and defensive lines)
1974-76	Calgary Stampeders (CFL), Assistant
	(Offensive and defensive lines)
1976	Calgary Stampeders (CFL), Interim head coach
1977-80	Calgary Stampeders (CFL), Assistant general manager
1980-82	Calgary Stampeders (CFL), Director of administration and player personnel
1983-86	Purdue, Assistant head coach
	(Defensive coordinator/defensive line)
1987-88	Wyoming, Assistant
	(Offensive coordinator/offensive line)
1989-90	Washington State, Assistant head coach
	(Offensive coordinator/offensive line)
1991-96	Wyoming, head coach
1997-present	Purdue, head coach

TILLER'S RANKING AMONG PURDUE COACHES

Bowl games

1. Joe Tiller, 8 (nine seasons)
2. Jim Young, 3 (three seasons)

Bowl victories

1. Joe Tiller, 3
1. Jim Young, 3

Overall victories

1. Jack Mollenkopf, 84 (14 seasons)
2. Joe Tiller, 67 (nine seasons)

Big Ten victories

1. Jack Mollenkopf, 57
2. Joe Tiller, 43

Overall winning percentage *

1. Noble Kizer, .750
2. Jack Mollenkopf, .670
3. Jim Young, .664
4. Joe Tiller, .609

* denotes minimum of five seasons

BIG TEN STANDINGS SINCE TILLER HAS BEEN PURDUE'S HEAD COACH

(1997-2005)

	Big Ten	Overall	Bowls
Michigan	58-14, .806	85-26, .766	9
Ohio State	51-21, .708	85-27, .759	8
Wisconsin	43-29, .597	77-37, .675	8
Purdue	43-29, .597	67-43, .609	8
Penn State	39-33, .542	65-43, .602	5
Iowa	38-34, .528	60-48, .556	6
Michigan State	32-40, .444	57-50, .533	4
Minnesota	29-43, .403	58-50, .537	6
Northwestern	27-45, .375	45-62, .421	3
Illinois	20-52, .278	37-66, .359	2
Indiana	16-56, .222	28-71, .283	0